Australia's
MOST NOTORIOUS
CONVICTS

BARBARA MALPASS EDWARDS

EXISLE
PUBLISHING

First published 2007

Exisle Publishing Limited
'Moonrising', Narone Creek Road, Wollombi, NSW 2325, Australia
P.O. Box 60-490, Titirangi, Auckland 0642, New Zealand
www.exislepublishing.com

National Library of Australia Cataloguing-in-Publication Data

Edwards, Barbara Malpass.
Australia's most notorious convicts.

Bibliography.
Includes index.
ISBN 9780908988884.

1. Convicts – Australia – History. 2. Convicts – Australia
– Case studies. 3. Australia – History – 1788–1851. I.
Title.

994.02

10 9 8 7 6 5 4 3 2 1

Designed by Christabella Designs
Typeset in Bembo 10/13
Printed in China through Colorcraft Limited, Hong Kong

CONTENTS

INTRODUCTION

Although Captain Cook's first voyage Down Under was, in the main, intended to plot the transit of the planet Venus, many people in authority believed that if England didn't find that mystical place supposedly to the east of New Zealand, then the French would. What Cook did find to the west of New Zealand, however, was the east coast of what became known, firstly, as New South Wales, and later Australia. His reports about one place, which he called Botany Bay, were optimistic.

During the next decade French explorers were very active in the Pacific region so it was decided that a settlement should be established to protect British interests. At the same time, England's American colonies had rebelled against British rule in the War of Independence, so would no longer accept the overflow of prisoners from English gaols. Sir Joseph Banks — an acknowledged expert on the Pacific region who had sailed with Cook — suggested that the prisoners could be sent to Botany Bay.

Settling this new land would lessen the effects of fast changes in English society by removing from England some of the dysfunctional people created by those changes. It would find new riches and develop the land; offer protection for the trade routes; and help England keep ahead in the empire-building game.

With the stored criminal population growing rapidly there was one result that still raises questions. Most of those punished by transportation, rather than death, managed to re-set themselves in a new place, but some had an urge to rebel and assault. Why? Did they seek to punish their tormentors by passing on the grief to simple folk less powerful than themselves? Why did some of that minority disappear into the mud and dust of time's repair and renewal processes? Why did some became headline news and attract crowds of strangers to watch their last performances on scaffolds and gibbets?

We have a lot of water and ground to cover while looking at these stories so, after we have thought for a moment about why the colony of New South Wales was established, we will take a brief trip through the widespread places where some convicts made their names and consider their claims to notoriety.

Chapter 1

THEY MUST HAVE HAD A REASON!

On 13 May 1787, the First Fleet set sail for Botany Bay in nine rented ships escorted by two naval vessels, carrying 759 convicts of whom approximately 25 died during the voyage. Amongst the others on board were three future governors, a medical group, an Anglican priest, a few more military administrators, four companies of marines (plus their wives and children), and sailors. For an expedition intended to set up a new colony, which would be self-supporting and eventually profitable, nobody had thought to include people skilled in farming or experts in the growth of flax. (Supposedly, one of the main reasons for the colony was the constant supply of good quality flax for the production of superior canvas for the navy's fleets.) There were no specially-commissioned master craftsmen on board and no basic farming equipment, such as a plough.

There are many reasons given for this curious voyage and those that followed, and the purposes behind them, so before we can look at some of the more questionable members of their cargoes, we need to look at why they were sent to *terra nullius* in the first place.

Population and economy

Up until the American War of Independence talk about settling the new Great South Land was just that, talk. There were good reasons to take it on — resources, such as flax for canvas and timber for building, were attractive to the navy, as was the idea of protecting trade routes to merchants. There were many more reasons for not doing so — distance, cost and unnecessary administrative problems. In addition, the problems of prisons and convicts being sent across the Atlantic could no longer be ignored. In the mid- to late-1700s, Britain was still a pre-industrial economy; there was a lot of money around, but development was not a general consideration except for personal gain, and in modern terms the economy was stagnant.

Only three cities outside of London had a population of around 25,000, and although places like Manchester were growing rapidly, only one in five of the total population lived in a large town. Early stages of the Agrarian Revolution dramatically changed farming practices. The development of machinery necessitated larger fields and hedges were dragged out and whole villages were flattened to accommodate the greater land blocks now needed for agriculture. The homeless, unemployed and unemployable, skilled and unskilled moved to the towns where the slums grew and the resources were stretched. Work in the cities was still restricted by guilds and the professions, so there was little employment to be found and the spread of income for any one year was very wide indeed. Making modern-day comparisons is difficult, but if we take the standard of one Australian dollar for one loaf of bread, then the rich could buy 70,000 loaves a year; a tradesman 1125 loaves a year; and the poor would have to survive on 152.5 loaves a year.

Poverty in Ireland was indescribable and some Irish migrants joined relatives in the north of England, cornering the market in the brute-strength work of digging canals ('navvies') and, eventually, laying tracks for the developing railway system. Added to this huge labour force and the hungry unemployed would be the unwanted public servants and soldiers sent home from the new America.

To steal a loaf of bread in such times could condemn one family to starvation; not to steal it could starve your own children. The simplest of crimes might earn a penny and a mug of gin would smother the pain of hunger. It was a frightening and dirty time and solutions were demanded.

The idea of transportation

Offenders have been banished from their home countries throughout time, partly to prevent their rise to hero status when they received extreme punishment but, in the main, because to be sent away from your own people was believed to dishonour them as much as the offender. After the American War of Independence, British felons had to stay home and unusable ships (hulks) became sleeping quarters for prisoners who were used for public labour during the day. These first hulks were operated by a private contractor who had been involved in the transportation of prisoners and bond servants to the Americas and was now, presumably, out of pocket. He was responsible for feeding, clothing and disciplining the convicts, but had no involvement in the public works for which they were used as unpaid labour.

Up until that point, transported men had been given money to establish a new life in America when their time was up, and a similar scheme worked with the hulks. This money was to be received in part by the prisoner on release and the remaining part on proof of a reputable life lived for some time in everyday society. Conditions were hard; rock breaking was considered work for the feeble and unwell and disease spread like wildfire in the overcrowded working conditions. Many did not live long enough to collect the money owed. Some boys as young as ten years of age were locked in the fetid hulks at night; at this time being a child was simply a stage in becoming able to serve society, and until you were old enough, herding geese and watching pigs was your apprenticeship.

The notion of adding convicts to the labour force of the faraway colonies, as a solution to Britain's overcrowded gaols and hulks, was now added to the debates about trade routes and empire building. One theme flowed through all discussions of crime and punishment — the punishment part must be 'continuous and rigid'; it must contain harsh discipline and endless labour. Juries may have been sympathetic enough to downgrade charges from hanging to incarceration offences, but the desperation and anger of the huge prisoner population must have hovered over every middle-class dinner table. Local high-ups and parliamentarians were pressured on all sides to 'do something'. But this must not be an easy 'out'.

What did they do?

The types of convicts changed over time as English penal law was eased. Although early charges included simple crimes such as minor theft, many sentences were gradually watered down by juries who didn't want to send criminals to their graves. As these laws changed many more serious crimes were also taken off the hanging sheet or were listed with transportation as an alternative and those set for transportation included the more professional criminals, such as the forger and the footpad — tougher creatures overall. Consequently the backgrounds of convicts stretched across society and while the majority had little education, some of those who decided to take the independent road of bushranging were recognised as being educated. There were some convicts whose records refer to specific trades and occupations, such as medicine and most building trade and professional skills.

Formal classifications of convicts crossed such divisions as age, crimes and gender. The major differentiation was the length of the sentence: seven years for simple robbery; fourteen years for theft of higher value goods; and life for anything more. Those whose sentences were still in place when slavery was abolished throughout the British Empire in 1834 were kept to their sentences, which probably shows that their sufferings were not considered to be unacceptable.

The stories of convict life are marked out by the punishments: being on the chain gang was just an extra load for the public service to be done; solitary confinement was an internal prison issue. Flogging was common throughout government and civil jurisdictions, so no eyebrows were raised to that (although the cat-o'-nine-tails used was not subject to the same regulations as those used in the army or navy), and hanging was an entertainment for many years — so both were facts of life. Food was awful and scarce for most of the convict population and in many ways convicts were back to the early days of civilisation: cold, hungry, brutalised and short-lived.

Classes of convicts included those who were described as being good enough to be granted tickets-of-leave, who could work for wages and had some carefully supervised freedoms; assigned servants who depended on their masters for everything; government servants; road gangs; hard-labour prisoners in chains (considered as the severest punishment 'man could inflict on man'); and those who had been convicted within the colony and served their time in the penal colonies and locals whose crimes earned them time in chains. Young boys were eventually categorised in separate establishments designed to provide inmates with the background for a productive and honest future, as well as providing the Great South Land with the necessary artisans it required.

So much of convict life was dependent on the goodness or otherwise of people with small or great power. No society can be stable if one person's wellbeing depends on another person's good nature and, as we will see, some of our desperate wanderers devoted a lot of their time to punishing those who injured the helpless.

What made a convict notorious?

Now that we have an idea of the kind of world that embraced and controlled convicts, we need to know what made some of them notorious. To do that we have to follow them along the path that colonial development followed. A huge crescent of power was pasted onto the corner of a continent with two attached islands that was called New South Wales. Journeys around this land were governed by curiosity, necessity and trade.

The convicts featured here were notorious for different reasons: some were personally attractive; their gentlemanly manners must have made the poorer of their victims feel good. Some tried to invent a Robin Hood reputation; being on the side of the poor settler against the local big nobs. A few were so horrible that they would make headlines even in the twenty-first century, and the urge to survive pushed some to extremes. All filled the newspapers and journals of the time with indignant columns blaming the authorities for neglect and inefficiency.

When working through the stacks of material on this group of people, we find that most official records refer to men only by their surnames, so whatever name they chose to give is the label they carry into history.

There were roughly three periods of bushranging: from 1788 to the 1840s with escaped convicts or bolters; the native-born bushrangers of the 1850s, sometimes the children of former convicts; and the gold-rush chancers, some up to the 1880s, with many being free settlers or the children of free settlers. All the notorious convicts we will meet in these pages were bolters: they ran and ran until they could run no more. Their lives were extreme; desperation was their touchstone. Crime was their career path — they were despised, dominated and insulted by the general population so, for some of them, regular folks became part of the enemy.

Chapter 2

AND WE'RE BOUND FOR BOTANY BAY

Sails flapped and yards creaked: the First Fleet arrived in Botany Bay and found it useless. The lie of the land meant there was no shelter for ships at anchor because the bay was too open. The water was shallow so that even fairly small ships could not pass beyond the entrance. Once landed, they found that on the low-lying ground the soil was of little value. Governor Arthur Phillip was expected to establish a settlement but, as a farmer, he knew that this would not do.

Phillip and two other officers travelled up the coastline, each commanding a long boat, checking out the bays on Captain Cook's charts. After two days they found a deep harbour with well-drained shores. As Philip Gidley King (who was shortly to become the founding commandant of Norfolk Island) recorded: 'Port Jackson was judged a very proper place.' So, they had finally arrived and amongst the 88 male convicts aboard the *Alexander* was John 'Black' Caesar — considered Australia's first bushranger.

John Caesar was born in about 1763, possibly in Madagascar, and may have been a slave in the West Indies before living in England where, in 1786, he got seven years' transportation for stealing money from a house. He stayed in the hulks until March 1787, when he joined the First Fleet.

He was obviously a hard and conscientious worker, but he was a big man with a big appetite for food as well as for work. Convict rations, even at their limited best, never satisfied him and in April 1789 his sentence was extended to a life term for stealing food.

Two weeks later Caesar stole weapons and ran for the bush. He was soon caught but escaped several more times and continued to be a local hero until he began robbing small settlers and raiding Aboriginal camps — all for food. Eventually he returned to base for help after being speared by Aborigines during one of his raids.

Severe shortages forced Governor Phillip to declare that stealing food from public stores would be a hanging offence. However, there were so many charges that most food thieves were flogged rather than executed and Caesar was one of those sent to Norfolk Island where he gained a little independence and supported himself on a small plot of land. Here he was allowed to keep a hog and eventually earned the use of one full acre (0.4 hectares). His daughter, Mary Anne, was born in March 1792 and when he was returned to Port Jackson a year later the baby and her mother, convict Ann Power, were left behind. (Mary Anne is recorded as travelling to Van Diemen's Land in 1813.)

After Caesar bolted again in July 1794, he was soon caught and again severely punished. He still declared he could not be 'made better'.

In 1795 he was with a working party that was attacked by a group of Aborigines led by the warrior leader, Pemulwuy. It was Caesar who injured Pemulwuy during the battle but the Aboriginal leader fled the hospital, despite belief that he would not survive.

Caesar escaped for the last time in December 1795 and led a band of absconders and wanderers around the Port Jackson area. The newly appointed Governor Hunter declared a reward of 5 gallons of rum for his capture in January 1796 and, less than two weeks later, Caesar was shot dead by John Wimbow at Liberty Plains (now Strathfield in Sydney).

John Caesar was not a very bad convict but, as a determined bolter whose defiance gained him public support, he offered a dream to the convict bushrangers of the next 50 years.

Setting the style

From 1796 onwards, records of what we would call bushranging are limited. In 1813 the *Sydney Gazette* reported that bushrangers 'infested' the outskirts of more distant settlements in New South Wales and in 1822 more than 30 men accused of bushranging were hanged. These men had mostly committed fairly petty, opportunistic crimes but complaints from the general population got louder as the villains got smarter, greedier and better organised.

Over the ensuing years the authorities and the bushrangers established their firm positions and most final encounters between the two were bloody and vengeful. It is probable that the experience of the Cumberland Gang made it impossible for either side to have any trust in the other.

In December 1824 Charles Patient, aged 21, was recorded as an absconder from Carters Barracks. He may have been back in custody in the following February but he must have bolted again because later in that same year he became the leader of the Cumberland Gang — a group that varied between six and ten men. The gang had a fearsome reputation, but very few real crimes were ever brought home to them. In the last six to eight weeks of their careers, the gang made raids on homes in

Cabramatta, South Creek, and on the Liverpool road. Patient would organise the women of the house in one room, where he would stand guard over them while the rest of the gang ransacked the place. He himself usually stole what books were available, reputedly searching for works by writers such as Scott and Byron, for amusement in the bush when they had 'nothing to do'.

The gang was popular amongst small settlers and, according to *The Australian*, they regularly visited Sydney on shopping trips. One member of the gang, Thomas Robinson, claimed that they had decided not to commit murder and that, if out-numbered, they would not fight when cornered. The newspaper considered this unlikely but, when the gang was betrayed, the story turned out to be true.

The Parramatta constables who were led to the gang's hideout had their muskets loaded, as did an elderly watchman. The gang were ordered to come out with their hands up, which they did. As they walked out each officer levelled his weapon at one of the bandits and fired. The watchman must have been an old hand who knew how to 'keep his powder dry' because in the soaking rain his was the only gun that worked. He killed one of the gang, a man named Nelson, and the rest raised their weapons now game for a fight, but by this time, the constables and the watchman had left the scene.

The idea that bushrangers would not surrender safely, no matter what deals were made, was quickly passed around and the end of the Cumberland Gang, after days of tracking and probably some local information, was recorded by *The Australian* with gusto, as references lingered around such gruesome details as protruding bowels and bloodied heads.

Eventually members of the gang, including Patient, Roberts, McCallum and Morrison, were convicted of 'putting

... persons in bodily fear' and sentenced to death. Thomas Robinson simply disappeared. They were hanged on 7 March 1826, less than a month after their capture. Corbett, an assigned convict, was charged with assisting the bushrangers to attack his master's house and was also condemned to death.

Governor Darling had introduced rewards for the betrayal of 'receivers': (people who took and sold stolen goods; sometimes those who harboured or abetted criminals). Those caught were forced to watch the deaths of the gang before being sent to Norfolk Island with no hope of remission.

The bold rebel

In Rolf Boldrewood's great Australian novel, *Robbery Under Arms*, published in 1882, the bushrangers' hideout is the 'Terrible Hollow'. This is described as a valley you would find through a shadowed gap in the high mountains where small farms prospered and cattle grazed. In real life this was 'The Camp' or 'The Shelter' in the Blue Mountains, a little over 50 miles (80.5 kilometres) from Sydney. For many decades, the site had been used by various outlaws as a secret hiding place to stash their loot or to recover from any injuries. Here stock ran wild and legends told of the authorities finding broken leg irons, rusted handcuffs and signs of terrible cruelties. The rubbish lying around included supposed proof of a well-told tale: this was about a man who was burned to death either because he was very stubborn or because the rumours of his hidden money were just that, rumours.

One group of outlaws that frequented The Camp was the Underwood Gang. Membership of the gang changed as bolters came and went, and one of those occasional members was Bold Jack Donohoe. Jack Donohoe was transported to New South Wales in 1824 for 'intent to commit a felony' and was assigned as a labourer to a Mr John Pagan at Parramatta. His very nature did him in. He was recorded as being disobedient and possessed a violent temper and was sent, chained, to the road gang at Vinegar Hill.

Donohoe was working on a pig farm in December 1827 when he and two companions, Smith and Kilroy, took some time off to hold up bullock teams and travellers on the Sydney to Windsor road. They were recognised by a traveller and all three were caught and condemned to death (twice apparently) on 1 March 1828. Donohoe escaped somewhere between the court and the gaol, but Smith and Kilroy were hanged along with two others in a stomach-clenching incident when Smith's rope broke. The governor ordered a stronger rope after he rejected pleas for mercy as Smith lay on the ground while his mate and the other two kicked out their last moments above him. The second time it worked but the *Sydney Gazette* was not impressed about the quality of materials being used: seemingly this wasn't the first time public money had been wasted in this way on inferior quality rope.

Donohoe moved into full-time bushranging and a £20 reward for his capture was posted. He often acted alone but for raids on bigger properties he joined up with other bushrangers and eventually joined up with Bill Webber and Jack Walmsley, and sometimes William Underwood would be with them. They generally went for wealthy landowners around Penrith, Liverpool, Windsor and Parramatta, but they also crossed the Blue Mountains and operated around Bathurst, occasionally sharing their plunder with poor settlers. It is even said that Donohoe and Underwood bailed up the flogging parson, Samuel Marsden, and liberated £4 from his purse.

Not generally violent, Donohoe's notorious bad temper gave him an edge when he demanded 'everything'. Courteous towards women, he still had no qualms about taking their belongings. When they held up a Mr Wilfred the 'everything' included his clothes — except for his shirt. Perhaps that is why Bold Jack's occasional nickname was 'The Stripper'! But he could also be sentimental. One planned raid was called off when Donohoe learned that the explorer Captain Charles Sturt, whom he much admired, was in the target house.

Like many other bushrangers Donohoe, Walmsley and Webber were fond of looking good. When they forced a merchant's dray off the road they spent so much time choosing their takings that the carters were able to give detailed descriptions of them. All three wore black hats, blue coats or trousers and 'plaited shirts' while Donohoe's snuff-coloured trousers topped good boots with worn toes.

In September 1830, Donohoe was shot in the head during a hearty battle at Bringelly, near Campbelltown, while he was cheering the others on. Webber was killed a month later and, when Walmsley was captured, his evidence sent more receivers to Norfolk Island.

In 1832, Underwood was shot dead. The story is that the gang found out he was keeping a diary with the intention of turning King's Evidence and he paid their price. Shortly after this, another member of the gang 'turned in' The Camp and the gang was finally broken up.

Bold Jack had stirred something amongst the people and curious things followed his death. Explorer Thomas Mitchell sketched the dead man, while a pipe maker was given permission to model Donohoe's head (including the bullet hole) to reproduce as clay tobacco pipes. A popular song about Donohoe ('The Wild Colonial Boy') was banned and hotels where it was heard were closed down. Yarns about popular bushrangers gave their heroes many names — but they often kept the initials B J D.

'Hang 'em in three days ...'

When Governor Darling came to office in 1826, bushrangers were more daring and getting cheekier. The new governor called on a mysterious character named Francis Nicholas Rossi to reform the police service. An aristocratic, Corsican-born head-kicker, and supposedly a secret agent with royal connections, Rossi arrived ahead of Darling to begin his main task, although one source records that Darling was one of those who refused to implement the major reform: the central control of all forces in an attempt to avoid local corruption. Seemingly it was Rossi who devised the laws for punishing anyone who supported bushrangers, forcing them to watch their mates at the end of a rope before they went to finish their own lives on Norfolk Island.

None of this really discouraged anyone desperate enough to take to the bush and in April 1830 the first act of a series called the *Bushranging Acts* was passed, proclaimed to take effect that same day. Its provisions were harsh: anyone could be arrested on suspicion of being an escaped convict and any arrested persons must prove their innocence. Anyone convicted of attacking homes was to be hanged within three days of sentencing (unless that third day was a Sunday, in which case they had to wait until Monday).

There were some strange results in the early days of the Act. The first Chief Justice of the Supreme Court of New South Wales, Francis Forbes, actually drafted it and urged its passing in the Supreme Court after landowner and politician John Blaxland was robbed in his own front yard. Forbes and Justice Dowling approved the Act against the view of the third judge on the tribunal.

One day when Forbes was walking near his property at Emu Plains, he was bailed up by a constable and had to prove his own identity. Justice Dowling, the second sponsor of the Act, was visiting John Blaxland when he himself was stopped on his way to work by an enthusiastic local constable. A wry joke, but no humour for Ralph Entwhistle, who was one of the first to be hanged under the strict provisions of the new law.

Entwhistle was transported for life in 1827 for stealing clothes and became an assigned man, driving a bullock team. One day in November 1829, Governor Darling and a large party were keeping an eye out for the Donohoe Gang as they rode along, so they probably didn't look into the water of the nearby Macquarie River where Entwhistle and a mate were cooling off. Unfortunately a very puritanical officer, Lieutenant Evernden, did look and sent troopers back to ensure the two were given 'the 50' for public indecency.

This incident is often recorded as the match that fired the Bathurst Insurgency, although it was probably lack of food that inspired the actions of the six men who absconded from a farm and forced other convicts to join them. Entwhistle became the leader of the band that grew with volunteers and 'conscripts' over time. To denote his authority he wore white ribbons around his hat and the gang became known as 'The Ribbon Boys'.

On 23 September 1830, The Ribbon Boys moved on to Woodstock Station, where they stole weapons and forced assigned servants to go with them. From there they moved on to a farm in Fitzgerald's Valley where an assigned man, Isaac Clements, had time to see that Entwhistle was armed with a shotgun before the boys locked him up. They eventually took Clements and the others along with them when they moved on to a property belonging to the well-remembered Evernden — Bartlett's Farm (now Wimbledon in the Cowra region) — where six of them, including Entwhistle, were recognised.

As usual they called on all the men to follow them, but one, Greenwood, refused and Entwhistle and two of his men fired at him from point blank range and again as he staggered towards the house, where he fell dead in front of the fireplace. By now nobody dared refuse to join The Ribbon Boys, but overnight one of the men from Bartlett's Farm, a man called Mack, escaped.

The gang now numbered up to 80 and the majority of them appear to have been dragged along rather than having waited to join a planned insurrection. After Greenwood's death, many followed Mack's example and snuck away.

The band continued to visit stations on their recruiting drive but their general behaviour was not vengeful and one owner stated that when the gang arrived at his place they took all his men — except one, whom they left to care for the sheep — and said they didn't wish to injure him as he was not a bad master. They took some tea, sugar, tobacco and all his blankets. From there they moved on to a property where they 'feasted', then on to another where they collected some horses.

By now the original gang realised that those they had coerced into joining them were not enthusiastic rebels; most were still sneaking away when they saw the chance. On Monday 27 September they had moved another 30 miles (48 kilometres), simply collecting food and ammunition. The following Friday they returned to Woodstock Station when, according to Isaac Clements, still an unwilling Ribbon Boy, most of the band went back to their home stations. One of the men who had been entrusted with the care of the ammunition slipped away and gave up their stores to the authorities.

Now Entwhistle told the few remaining conscripts that they were free to go home and they did, leaving behind an ominously counted thirteen — well armed and well mounted.

Of that thirteen, ten would survive for trial.

The Bathurst Hunt Club organised a posse — some of its members being 'substitutes' for the less robust affiliates of the club — and twelve of them were chosen for the action. More armed men were sent from Sydney and battles were fought up and around the hills, always on the run and always to the advantage of The Ribbon Boys, who were reputed to have an experienced strategist in their midst.

Some reports say that, sensing defeat, the gang surrendered at Shooter's Hill, while another tells of a dramatic three-day shoot-out at Abercrombie Caves that lasted until the remaining ten surrendered.

In the Supreme Court, sitting at Bathurst on 30 October, all were sentenced to death and hanged within the obligatory three days: the first public execution in Bathurst.

But they didn't go away

The new Act's authority of arrest without warrant, along with the three-day hanging law, may have reduced the incidence of bushranging for a few years. As if to prove that no one was free of the convict's hand, one notable event in 1834 was the murder of barrister and former editor of *The Australian* Robert Wardell, who was effective, along with Wentworth, in establishing the significant concept of freedom of the press.

Wardell had a herd of deer on his property and one day came across a group of bolters — John Jenkins, Thomas Tattersdale and one other, probably a man called Emanuel Brace, who eventually turned King's Evidence. The three were butchering one of the animals and Wardell threatened to have them flogged. Jenkins drew his gun and when Wardell turned his horse to get away, Jenkins shot him in the back. Jenkins and Tattersdale were caught and sentenced to death after Jenkins threatened to shoot the bunch of unmentionable idiots who comprised the court and physically attacked Tattersdale in the dock.

And still they came. William Roberts was an accredited cooper — a maker of barrels. Here we have a picture of a brawny apron–clad man using a heavy hammer to ram rings of hot metal down around the barrel staves: perhaps that is why he was known in his few bushranging months as 'Jack (or Billy) the Rammer'.

When transported for seven years for stealing a bucket, Roberts left behind a wife and three children. He arrived in Sydney in September 1833 and was assigned to the property Ginninderry, owned by George T Palmer. (That land is now part of the national capital, its name remembered in a creek, a large lake and a major road.)

Roberts escaped in 1834 but was recaptured and sent to Goulburn Gaol. Here he met and escaped with Joseph Keys who'd been transported for highway robbery in April 1829, landing in Sydney in 1830. He too had escaped, was recaptured and sent to Goulburn Gaol. The two travelled to the Monaro district in New South Wales where they met up with Edward Boyd.

Boyd, also a seven years' man, was assigned to a station at the junction of the Maclaughlin and Snowy rivers, but bolted and met up with Roberts and Keys. At one of their earlier raids, at Coolringdon Station, owned by the senior government official Stewart Ryrie, a sword was stolen. When the group was finally captured some months later, possession of that sword was taken as proof of Boyd's early involvement with Roberts and Keys.

From 2 September to 14 December 1834 the group was damned for 'terrorising the Monaro'. After the earlier raids they turned up in mid-December at Rock Flat, just south of

Cooma. They held up part-owner Joseph Catterall and his wife Georgiana — who was quite heavily pregnant and became very frightened. The gang took everything of value, including all ammunition but birdshot. They destroyed all the weapons except convict overseer Charles Fisher Shepherd's shotgun — because he taught Roberts how to use a compass.

The gang returned around dawn, now intending to flog Shepherd who, as well as boasting that he wasn't afraid of them, had had one of his convicts given 'the 50' on the property instead of referring the matter to the appropriate magistrate. Shepherd had already loaded his shotgun in preparation for their return, and killed Roberts. He himself was wounded several times and received another shot at close range before being left for dead. (A neighbour carted Shepherd to Goulburn, where he recovered.)

In January 1835 a party of troopers caught up with the remaining duo alongside the Snowy River. They tried to swim across but Boyd was shot by one of the troopers. Keys escaped, but the troopers placed a watch on all the stations in the area, and a few days later Trooper Smith caught Keys at Jimenbuen Station.

In May 1835, Keys was tried in Sydney on a charge of attempted murder. He pleaded guilty and was hanged on 2 June. Also tried was Thomas Pearson on a charge of aiding and abetting Keys. Pearson, a convict from the Rock Flat Station, was also sentenced to death, but was transported to Norfolk Island for life.

Move 'em, damn 'em, move 'em

Convicts were considered 'non-persons' and could be moved around at will. Martin Cash (tuck his name into the corner of your mind for later) and William Westwood best display this out-of-control life to which they were condemned.

William Westwood who, folk said, spoke in dictionary words and must have been educated, earned the reputation of a 'gentleman bushranger' and records show that he had strong views about behaviour towards others. He had already served a sentence for highway robbery when he was transported to Australia for stealing a coat in 1837 and was assigned to a property in the Goulburn district (possibly that of Mr Phillip Parker King, the son of the former governor). The overseer there had a reputation for brutality and after three years Westwood bolted with the violent Paddy Curran. Their first independent act was to return to the station and give the overseer 'the 50' with his own whip.

Like the overseer, Curran was a bully and during a raid on Dr Murphy's property at Woden (today part of Canberra), Westwood, by now known as Jackey Jackey, took Curran's horse and rifle and chased him away after he attacked one of the women. (Curran was later arrested for rape and murder and was hanged at Berrima Gaol in September 1841.)

It's good to get a woman's view on male-defined gentlemanly behaviour. At one time Westwood had a cave hideout on Black Mountain — just across the plain from the current Federal Parliament House — and nearby was a sly grog shanty run by a woman called Julia Webb, who would know good men and bad inside and out. In Julia's opinion, Westwood really was one of Nature's best.

Almost up to the end Westwood held to his ideas of just and unjust and never hesitated to spread the word. A large property on Canberra's Limestone Plains was run by William Klensendorlffe, an unpopular man and keen bushranger catcher. By November 1824, he had captured five of them and was probably eager to collect one as well known as Westwood.

When Westwood robbed one of Klensendorlffe's assigned men, the enraged martinet set out to what is now known as Kingston. There he raced around on his favourite mare and picked on a wandering man, demanding if he had seen anything of a bushranger. As he looked down from his fine horse Klensendorlffe saw not a pair of eyes but a pair of gun barrels. Then he lost his chestnut mare, his favourite pistol and his clothes. After receiving a lecture about the treatment of his fellow humans, he was allowed to march homeward in his flannel underpants. More than one person (and not only convicts) thought it a pity he had been released.

Westwood generally moved around the Bungendore, Tarago, Boro and Braidwood regions holding up coaches and travellers and collecting money, watches and other fancies, as well as picking up the money collected at the tollgates. After farewelling Klensendorlffe he set out to spend Christmas at a camp in the hills around Bungendore. He visited an old friend and sent him to Bungendore's Harp Inn to buy some Christmas cheer. Westwood was bored during his friend's long trip and went out for a walk. From a patch of higher ground he saw his Christmas goodies racing towards him — in the company of five armed constables. Westwood hid and snuck away on foot back to his camp, sorry to leave his beautiful chestnut horse behind. Thinking Bungendore might be a little crowded he moved on towards Braidwood.

In January 1841, after robbing a store at Boro Creek, he was caught when chasing another potential victim into Bungendore. He explained that his horse was worn out and his gun wouldn't fire, then he spent the next two days escaping and being caught. Locked in a room at the local inn, he jumped through a window (it was closed at the time) but was caught again; next day, on the road to Sydney, he escaped again and went back to business causing a new reward of £30 to be offered for his capture. Back in Berrima in April 1841 he was recognised by the innkeeper's daughter who grabbed him and screamed for help. A carpenter working nearby offered help by hitting Westwood on the head with a hammer.

On 15 April 1841 Westwood was tried at Berrima Court House for robbery with firearms and sentenced to penal servitude for life. En route to Sydney he escaped from the Stonequarry (Picton).

During this escape he bailed up a carriage pulled by a couple of good-looking horses. The owner of this carriage was Mr Francis McCarty — the magistrate who had condemned him in Berrima. He borrowed one of the horses and watched the coach driver, from a nearby hill, encourage the remaining horse, while Mr McCarty pushed from the rear. Recaptured in July he was held on Cockatoo Island until sent to Van Diemen's Land, arriving on 8 March 1842, which is where we will meet him again.

A sentimental gang

Many bushrangers had curious attitudes and naive sentimentalities. In December 1838, Thomas Whitton and Archibald Thompson (Scotchie) were supposed to be involved in the murders at Redfern Station but no more was heard of them until September 1839, when they were joined by Russell. In September that year, along with the fourth member of the group, Bernard Reynolds, they set out on a series of crimes, which earned them the title 'our bloodiest bushrangers'.

One evening, during the annual cattle muster, fourteen men settled down for their pipe and chat. Whitton and his three mates arrived and threatened to kill the first to move. They took everything of value and while they were busy the manager suggested to one of his companions that they could fight them off. The other man was an ex-convict and the idea went nowhere. Several days later the manager was telling his wife and friends about how guns could make cowards of them all when the gang walked through the front door. Scotchie ordered them all outside but the manager's wife stayed behind and begged him not to take away all they had because they were newly married. Scotchie was impressed and possibly sentimental and called off his three mates and left.

Some time later the manager moved on to another of the owner's properties and one evening the door of the house was hammered on, along with a yell of 'Police'. When he opened the door there were Scotchie, Whitton and Russell, guns at the ready. Again Scotchie was moved to generosity to the extent of leaving one gun behind (after supper) so that the wife could protect herself whenever her husband was away. A neighbour was not so lucky.

This neighbour had been a convict constable with a reputation of being a tough boss. Also newly married, he boasted he wasn't afraid but when Scotchie and the boys arrived he stayed inside and fired from a window. The gang responded and the wife was injured. The gang collected everything they could before making the wife comfortable. She recovered but was left with a limp.

In January 1840 the *Australasian Chronicle* complained that no one in the Lachlan region was safe from this group; that even though the Legislative Council taxes were paying for all kinds of police, not one of those listed had been able to capture Scotchie and Whitton during their three-year rampage.

On Sunday 19 January the group attacked Oak Park near Crookwell: they were looking for Francis Oakes, a former Chief Constable of the Parramatta district. Told that everyone was watching a field being reaped, they marched along there. According to one witness they threatened to set the wheat field on fire and burn everyone in it. One assigned servant, John Hawker, was shot but Francis Oakes and his brother escaped to a nearby property. Tired of searching for the brothers, the gang drove everyone back to the house and set it on fire. When they ordered a groom to bring up horses they found that the terrified animals wouldn't come near the burning house.

After that, on Monday 20 January, they moved on to a property at Gunning intending to attack the pub. From a neighbouring property Mr John Hume, brother of explorer Hamilton Hume, heard the gunfire and went to help. When asked who he was he responded by asking them who they were and their answer was three bullets. The gang was reported as having 'detained his body for some hours' before it was returned to his family.

After Gunning their next project was killing a Mr Oliver Fry, who ran Narrawa Station at the Fish River. Although the resulting court actions do not explain the reasons for this attack, Mr Fry's actions when he saw the men arrive suggest that he knew who they were and what they wanted.

He had just enough time to barricade himself inside his hut. The gang settled into the stable and the two-hour gun battle began. The attackers left suddenly and blood was found in the stable. It was Scotchie who had been wounded and either he shot himself or Whitton kept to a long-standing agreement of death before capture and finished him off. Whitton and the two other men carried Scotchie's body away, finally throwing it into a nearby river.

A few days later a police party came across the bushrangers at morning tea. All took shelter behind nearby trees and eventually the gang surrendered. Russell had been wounded and, when the police approached, he put his small pistol to his mouth and kept the old bond. Whitton and Reynolds were taken to Goulburn Gaol, but Russell had the last laugh on the journey. His body hadn't been properly tied onto his horse and when it fell off officers had to retrace several kilometres before finding him. It seems nothing could keep Russell from bolting.

Reynolds, too, kept his part of the old bargain. His sister had brought him some clean shirts to wear in court and he wrapped them around the chains on his ankles. That way, when he hanged himself with a noose made from blankets, his feet didn't clank on the door and alert the warders.

Whitton was charged with the murder of John Hawker at Oak Park and the charge of murdering John Hume was kept in reserve. He was hanged within a metre of his prepared grave after a parade and speeches.

Returning to the old ways

Sometimes when people change their names for anonymity or to protect their families they still hold on to the thought of something they really value. The man we meet next kept his Jewish faith to the very bitter end.

In 1832 a man later known as Edward Davis (leader of the Jewboy Gang) stood trial at the Old Bailey as George Wilkinson and received a sentence of transportation for seven years for theft. He arrived in Sydney in February 1833 and worked at the Hyde Park Barracks until he escaped that December. Caught and sentenced to an extra year, he escaped again and received another twelve months.

Assigned to a farmer at Hexham he ran away for a third time in January 1837 and two more years were added to his sentence — and he was caught again. In July 1838 he ran away for the fourth time and stayed away.

He began to make his name as Davis when in January 1839 he formed a bushranging gang in northern New South Wales. For two years this gang travelled from Maitland to the New England ranges, the Hunter Valley and down to Brisbane Waters near Gosford. They established their headquarters in the hills south of Dungog and from there made sudden raids on townships or settlements or raced down to ambush any travellers they spied on the road. Everything that happened in the area at the time was attributed to what people called 'the Jewboy Gang' and Davis became known as an Australian Robin Hood when he took everything from the rich and went out of his way to offer help to assigned servants.

In 1840 the gang concentrated on the Quirindi, Tamworth and Maitland districts and by the end of that year there were seven of them; six were known — Edward Davis, John Shea, John Marshall, John Everett, Robert Chitty and Richard Glanville. The seventh man was never officially named (although one source refers to him as James Bryant), and he escaped during the final stand-off.

One text considers them to be more your rowdy juvenile delinquents than hardened criminals. They had a fanciful idea of themselves as gentlemen, with their gaudy, stylish yet stolen clothes and the pink ribbons they tied to the bridles of their thoroughbred horses, also stolen. The Jewboy Gang was popular in the country. They were reasonably courteous to victims who had no record of abusing their assigned men. But they 'tried' and flogged an overseer with a harsh reputation. They robbed a chief constable and his men, taking all their money, all their weapons, plus more clothes and horses, leaving behind a group of men who suffered nothing more than severe embarrassment.

Davis was also friendly with the local Aborigines and an Aboriginal girl was often seen with the gang, reloading guns and guarding victims during robberies.

Through all their encounters they had never killed and Davis always swore that extreme violence was only for extreme situations. It was almost inevitable that one day a member of the public or a member of the gang would panic or lose his nerve.

Just before Christmas in 1840, they reached Scone and divided their labours. Davis, Everett and Glanville went to bail up the St Aubin Arms while Shea, the unknown seventh man, Chitty, and Marshall set out to rob Dangar's Store. Here the new chum clerk, John Graham, fired a shot and Shea fired back. Graham was killed and the gang made a dash for Doughboy Hollow near Murrurundi in the Liverpool Ranges. A posse of settlers and ticket-of-leave men attacked. Davis was wounded in the shoulder and the whole gang, except for the seventh member, was captured and taken to Sydney for trial.

In the Supreme Court, Shea was charged with murder and Davis and the others with aiding and abetting him. Davis and his companions were found guilty, even though they weren't present during the killing. Chief Justice Dowling, one of the keenest sponsors of the *Bushranging Act*, sentenced them all to death.

Public sympathy for Davis was strong but the sentences were all confirmed and carried out on 16 March 1841. Witnesses at the executions claimed that Davis was the only repentant man amongst them and he was buried in the Jewish portion of the Devonshire Street cemetery. He seems to have been the only Jewish bushranger in Australia, whoever he really was.

Really, really bad

Of all the bushrangers and their crimes John Lynch stands out as a truly bad and disturbed man. He claimed nine murders, although the police believed there was a tenth, all with an axe and all — but the 'unlucky' one — with one blow.

In 1831 Lynch was transported for robbery on the same ship as his father who had been convicted of manslaughter. When he killed Kearns Landregan with two blows of his axe, instead of the customary one, he broke his luck, at least that was his explanation for the end of the life he had murdered to create.

Lynch first worked on a road gang near Berrima before receiving a ticket-of-leave with the help from a Mr Mulligan. He was suspected of being involved in the murder of another convict but the only available witness was too drunk to stand up in court so Lynch was set free. When he was charged with regularly harbouring bushrangers he ran for cover to Mr Mulligan's property at Wombat, where he was allowed to stay.

On 19 February 1841 a Mr Tinney and his driver parked their bullock dray overnight at Ironstone Bridge, near Mittagong. The next morning the driver walked along the creek collecting the bullocks back to work. He saw a pile of newly cut scrub and was curious. He pulled the branches aside and found a body — one that had died very violently. The driver went into Berrima and brought back police, a magistrate and a doctor. Searching the area they found signs of a small fire and some freshly strewn hay, presumably to feed the camper's horse. Grey horse hairs were found where the animal had rolled.

A man identifying himself as John Dunleavy, who had taken over the Wombat farm from Mulligan, had bought goods at the Berrima Post Office and the White Horse Hotel and had changed a £5 note. It was noticed that his cart was drawn by a grey horse, and the horse was noticed again when he stopped at the Woolpack Inn for an evening meal.

The body was identified by some medals around the neck as Landregan and the number on the £5 note spent in Berrima was identified as part of his savings which he had been carrying. When last heard of he had sent a message to his wife saying that he had found work doing fencing for a Mr Dunleavy.

Mr Chalker, landlord of the Woolpack Inn and Chief Constable Chapman and Sergeant Freer went to Mulligan's farm. Here a man acknowledged as Dunleavy was identified as John Lynch and declared to be 'a prisoner illegally at large'.

Finally people started asking questions about the whereabouts of the Mulligans — both Mr and Mrs along with their teenage son and young daughter. A letter supposedly from Mulligan in Wollongong was checked and the writing declared fake.

Lynch was tried and when condemned finally confessed to some of his crimes along with the list of deeply felt resentments he considered justification for his actions. He complained about life's unfair treatment: how he had been declared a lifer when his sentence had really been only seven years; how he had applied for his papers but had been kept waiting without reason; how Mulligan (his 'fence' of choice) had cheated him when he brought stolen goods to him for selling on; and how he only stole some bullocks to sell for money for a fresh start. Then he told about the killings.

At Mount Razorback he had met a carter and a young Aboriginal boy who was taking care of the animals. The carter was Mr Ireland and his animals earned care because they hauled a valuable load. Lynch thought he could make something of that load and he disposed of Mr Ireland and the boy — each with a single blow. He explained how, when he met Mr Cowper, the owner of the goods, in Liverpool, he told him that Mr Ireland was sick and that the Aboriginal boy was caring for him. He gave every detail of his arrangements to meet Mr Cowper in Sydney to deliver the goods; and told how he himself sold the goods — as if it was the most natural thing in the world.

Things did become a little complicated for him when, driving Mr Ireland's dray, he met Mr Frazer and his son and they travelled together for a while. He may have enjoyed that part of his trip; driving along with mates, sharing carting stories with father and son. When they stopped for a breather Lynch rested under the dray and to the trooper who stopped to pass the time of day, everything must have looked fine; father, son and two drays — an enviable life. The trooper asked about whom they had met on the road but they didn't think to mention the man resting under the dray. Now the Frazers had to go — and they did, each with a single blow — and their dray moved on with Lynch.

Then off to Mulligans' place where he demanded the money he believed was owed to him. All four of the Mulligans got the single blow and the bodies were burnt. Now Lynch established himself as Dunleavy, the new owner of the Wombat farm. He advertised in a newspaper as Mr Mulligan, declaring he was no longer responsible for Mrs Mulligan's debts because she had left him; he wrote to Mulligan's debtors, as Mulligan, telling of the sale and promising that this new Mr Dunleavy would pay all the debts.

For six months he played the part and won local sympathy for being, in popular opinion, overcharged for the property. Then he told of how he went to Sydney and on the way met the talkative Landregan and his money and how he broke his luck forever with the double blow.

Lynch was hanged in April 1842 at Berrima Gaol. He was 22 years old. According to one source his skull is in the Australian Museum in Sydney.

Chapter 3

ACHIEVING HELL ON EARTH

Six weeks after the First Fleet arrived in Botany Bay the British flag was raised on Norfolk Island. Under the command of Lieutenant Philip Gidley King were some settlers, some freemen and fifteen convicts. Apart from the usual desire to stop the French expanding their empire, there were two other reasons for this new settlement: the island's timber and the flax for the maintenance of the navy, and the need for an abundant vegetable garden for the mainland settlers whose supplies were short and not of very good value.

After a quarter of a century the island was empty. Manufactured goods, such as buildings and bridges, were either flattened or broken apart. All domesticated animals were slaughtered and the dogs were left wild to fend for themselves. This new peace lasted eleven years until it was decided that Norfolk Island should be brought back to some kind of life again. For the next 30 years Norfolk Island became, quite deliberately, the nadir of convict degradation. Intended to be the closest thing to death, the new settlement made Hell desirable.

Most visitors to the island, both the official and the merely curious, refer in their tales to the prisoner Michael Burns with a kind of admiring horror. An example of the 'success' achieved by the harsh regime and listed as 'quiet and submissive', Burns had spent months at a time in the dark, months at a time on bread and water, and had received a staggering 2210 lashes.

Then there was Van Diemen's Land. Apart from keeping out the French there were other reasons for settling here. These included the Huon pine for shipbuilding and the coal for general development that were discovered around Macquarie Harbour in 1815. Prison settlements were established around 1804 for convicts in Sydney who had committed extra offences and by 1818 it was officially labelled a 'place of banishment' as well as a valuable resource and from 1822 other settlements began to grow.

As with the first settlements around Sydney, lack of food became a major problem. At one stage only the arrival of a whaleboat willing to give up its supplies saved the settlement from starvation. So severe was the situation that convicts were allowed weapons to hunt kangaroos. Some returned, some did not, but for settlers too a convict's hunting prowess was a life saver. Some of the bolters found that kangaroo meat and the occasional side of mutton could be exchanged with the settlers for dry rations and gun powder.

The Vandemonians

Many thousands passed through Van Diemen's Land's convict system. Of the first five bolters who skipped in 1806 only Richard Lemon, Antill (sometimes referred to as Scanlon) and Brown were listed by name. Things were difficult for Lemon because Antill and Brown spoke Gaelic, which Lemon did not understand and he was sure that they were talking about him all the time with no fond interest. He solved that problem by killing Antill as he drank from a pond (now named after him). That doesn't seem to have discouraged Brown because, odd as it may seem, he and Lemon were still travelling together in 1808 when, in a place now carrying Lemon's name, they met up with a Mr Mansfield. Mr Mansfield is recorded in one report as a bounty hunter who had heard that there were rewards of £50 on each of their heads and that he collected Lemon's head, along with the reward, by forcing Brown, at gunpoint, to cut it off before taking Brown and the trophy back to Hobart Town where he claimed the reward then took Brown to Government House where he received a free pardon for helping bring in his mate.

Many who escaped disappeared from sight, like John Green and Joseph Saunders, who made a break for it on 4 March 1822. They (and their pursuers) were never seen again. That didn't stop another six trying their luck within the week. A few, like James Goodwin and Thomas Connell, survived tremendous journeys around and across the region and brought back valuable information for the authorities. Some, as we shall see, stayed away — for a while at least.

An individual view

Michael Howe spent two years in the merchant navy off Yorkshire's bleak coast before deserting to join the Royal Navy. When he was nineteen he dumped the navy life to join the army and then deserted it too. Seemingly allergic to authority he tried out an independent lifestyle as a highwayman, which resulted in his journey, in 1812, to the very authoritarian Van Diemen's Land.

Once again he departed without formalities and in 1813 joined another convict called John Whitehead, who had organised one of the first multi-skilled gangs. Howe became chief lieutenant of this gang, which (according to one source) consisted of up to 28 deserters and convicts. The gang's policy of punishing landholders who had abused their assigned convicts earned them sympathy from small settlers who helped them with food and information about police in the area. During a battle with the 46th Regiment, Whitehead was killed and Howe took his head away so that the soldiers could not collect the reward. He then assumed leadership of the gang.

When in May 1814 an amnesty was offered to bushrangers who surrendered before December, many of Howe's gang took the offer, but early in the following year Howe had put together a more organised gang. They ransacked the New Norfolk settlement on the Derwent River, taking everything people owned, after which they operated a violent protection racket amongst the settlers. Court reports include tales of senseless killings, which probably helped enforce the gang's authority.

Much as Howe disliked being subjected to authority, he loved being an authority himself. He organised members of the gang like a ship's crew and ordered them to call him 'Admiral'. One source says he declared himself, 'Lieutenant-Governor of the Woods', and another refers to him as, 'Governor of the Rangers', however all say he wrote to Lieutenant-Governor Thomas Davey, demanding, amongst other things, a pardon if he surrendered.

Gang fatalities were high and Howe decided to move on again. By now he was travelling with his companion, Mary Cockerill, an Aboriginal girl who was seen at many raids. Mary was heavily pregnant when they were making a run for it, either leaving the gang behind or escaping from a group of searchers. It was probably an accident but, as he turned and fired at pursuers, Howe shot Mary. Accident or not she was keen to see him captured and gave up what information she had.

A little later he offered to take up new Lieutenant-Governor William Sorell's offer of a pardon and he spent some time in Hobart Town socialising and threatening anyone who tried to stand in his way in any situation. He heard a rumour that the pardon would not be coming and fled again.

One night he was surprised in the bush by two men, Watts and Drew, who believed they could collect the new reward on his head. Howe knifed Watts and shot Drew with Watts' gun. Watts was able to crawl away and, when found, was able to give information about where Howe might be found.

Eventually a kangaroo shooter, a soldier and a seaman found Howe and beat him to death. He was buried on the spot but his head was taken to Hobart for exhibition.

When found, Howe's body was wearing kangaroo skins. He was keeping a diary covered in kangaroo skin, using kangaroo blood as ink. He was writing about the flowers of his native Yorkshire and his wish to grow them in his planned mountain hideout.

His name is remembered in a marshland and in a gully on the Derwent River. A pamphlet written about him by Thomas Wells referred to him as 'the last and worst' of bushrangers. In 'worst' he had competitors and 'last' he was not.

Food for survival

Tales of cannibalism, the final desperate clinging to life with nothing to stand in the way, were regularly spun around, but only a few were ever recorded. A suspected case in 1824 faded away after the original investigation: four convicts bolted and three were recaptured. They all swore that the fourth had died but, when their described journey was backtracked, his bloodstained clothing was found and, rammed into the ground nearby, were three sharpened sticks. Around the sharp ends of the sticks were patches of dried blood with what looked like shreds of flesh sticking to them.

In 1825 ten men made a run for it early in March. One was picked up in April and he told his captors that he had fled from the others because they were drawing lots on whom to eat.

Five years later a better-documented story came along. Six prisoners had bolted between 1 and 3 September 1830; one was caught in less than a week and two, Broughton and McAvoy, were captured in October. They gave evidence that Coventry and Hutchinson had gone their separate ways soon after leaving Macquarie Harbour and that Feagan had been 'killed by natives'. Condemned to hang, Broughton and McAvoy made their last confessions the night before their executions.

Broughton had the job of killing Hutchinson and the remaining four shared him; Feagan tried to kill Coventry but needed help to finish the job; then finally, McAvoy killed Feagan. Two days later the last two, Broughton and McAvoy, found some dogs pulling down a kangaroo so they took that meat and left the last of Feagan behind.

Until these confessions there was no confirmation of such actions, although the tale of Matt Gabitt had been recorded some years before. Declared one of the worst of the early bushrangers, Gabitt and a few others escaped from Macquarie Harbour in 1822. It was agreed that Gabitt should lead the group and they robbed travellers and raided lone settlements until no one would help them any more. They were soon short of food and Gabitt organised a butchering party. Being the sole survivor of the group, it was assumed he had eaten the rest — mainly because he was carrying part of an arm when he surrendered himself at Macquarie Harbour. He was hanged. Such a short, almost dismissive, account in the records perhaps because, before then, there had been Alexander Pierce.

Pierce was a pickpocket sentenced to seven years' transportation. Between May and November 1821 he was given 150 lashes for various crimes and was sent to Macquarie Harbour — intended to be the most extreme penal settlement in the colony. In September 1822, he was one of seven prisoners (Thomas Bodenham, James Brown, Bill Cornelius, Alexander Dalton, Alexander Pierce, John Mathers and Matthew Travers), who stole a boat at Kelly's Basin and picked up a man named Bob Greenhill who was to be their navigator.

When they saw signal fires ashore they left the boat and went bush where they ended up in such a state that Cornelius was reported as being so hungry he would be willing to eat some of a man. That idea was taken up by the group and one of their number, Alexander Dalton, who had offered himself as a flogger whilst in prison, was deemed appropriate to be first on the block. That night Greenhill killed him and the men feasted on his heart and liver.

The next day two of the band, Cornelius and Brown, gave themselves up and died in hospital. The remaining five struggled on and killed Bodenham and dried the meat before travelling further. It was Mathers' turn next and he was given time to say his prayers; then Travers took the blow. Only Greenhill and Pierce were left now and they daren't sleep — but Pierce stayed awake longest and killed Greenhill.

When captured some weeks later in company with two old acquaintances, Pierce was keen to tell his tale. The authorities believed the bit about the 250 sheep he had stolen and about the robberies at a number of stations, but the rest of his story was considered fanciful and he was sent back to Macquarie Harbour and the other two were hanged.

In November 1823 he escaped again, taking Thomas Cox with him this time. When retaken he claimed that the body parts he was carrying were simply to prove that Cox was dead and, as he did have regular bread and salted meat with him, he clearly wasn't starving. When Cox's body was found the meatier parts were missing and his head and hands had been discarded. Pierce was hanged in July 1824.

Not a good word was heard

Bushranging tales and formal records vary in terms of blame, needs and desperation, but one thing most seem to agree on is the outstanding awfulness of Mark Jeffries. Jeffries was condemned in Scotland but was reprieved when he volunteered to act as a flogger and hangman and when he arrived in the colony in 1822 he became a scourger. He was reputedly a drunk who blamed all his faults on the demon grog. He was drunk while trying to abscond with a female prisoner from a watch-house he was guarding, and claimed it wasn't his fault. But he was flogged anyway and eventually sent to Macquarie Harbour for threatening a constable with a knife. In 1825 he bolted with two other men named Hopkins and Russell. They survived for a while but when they ran out of ammunition and food they decided to toss for it. Russell lost and Jeffries shot him immediately. Russell fed them for five days until they found some sheep and discarded the last of him. They took up bushranging and, while Hopkins left little or no record, Jeffries moved into the Brady Gang for a while, but was kicked out for molesting women.

He was acting independently when he attacked the Tibbs home. He ordered a stockman and Mr and Mrs Tibbs, along with their new baby, to go into the bush with him. The stockman refused and was shot out of hand. Struggling through the bush Jeffries complained because Mrs Tibbs wasn't walking fast enough. Apparently she said it was because of carrying the baby; Jeffries took the baby by the heels and smashed its head against a tree. Mr Tibbs rushed at him and was shot. Jeffries moved on leaving Mrs Tibbs with her dead baby and dying husband.

Moving on to Georgetown he robbed a Mr Baker and then forced him to act as a porter. Mr Baker obediently trudged along with Jeffries, who prodded him from behind. Suddenly Jeffries shot Mr Baker, retrieved his pack from the body and moved on.

Captured by John Batman, who was a very effective seeker after bushrangers at that time, Jeffries was taken into town. Contemporary reports claimed that his arrival nearly caused a riot. He was hanged in April 1826.

'A Manchester man'

All the nightmare escape tales in the world would not deter some. One of the most successful was that engineered by Matthew Brady in 1824. Brady was transported in 1820 — either for forgery or for stealing bacon and dairy goods (depending on the source). In his first four years as a convict he was given up to 350 lashes for trying to escape and for being a general nuisance. Transferred to Macquarie Harbour in 1824 he met more like-minded men and led a successful run for freedom.

According to which source you read, Brady and fifteen (or five) fellow prisoners stole a boat, which had delivered a logging crew to Kelly's Basin. Among the group were Patrick Bryant, John Burns, James Crawford, Patrick Connolly and James McCabe. They tied up those who refused to join them and set sail. There must have been at least one man in the group with small-boat experience because they sailed the dangerous waters around to the mouth of the Derwent before going ashore and establishing their reputation for style, determination and Brady's courteous treatment of women.

An early attack was on the property called Clarendon. Brady and several of the gang came ashore and persuaded a stockman to show them the route to the house. Leaving a couple of men to watch the approach road they took over everything. A new batch of bread, freshly prepared bacon and hams, butter and milk were collected from the dairy. They had a meal and filled up their packs with food before ransacking the house and politely bidding everyone farewell, after which they warned the group not to raise the alarm for at least half an hour and tied a few folk to some trees. Those people were lucky; there was someone around to release them — on other occasions some died before being found.

The loot from one robbery, at Swansea in 1825, was found buried later. During that robbery they had stolen a whaleboat as transport. For some reason they forced a man to go with them and, according to one report, he was killed in a drunken orgy.

They spent two years in this way but, according to a Mr Lloyd who recorded his travels in the colonies some years later, Brady was 'the most mercifully disposed of all Van Diemen's Land's villains'.

Their most dramatic exploit was the takeover of a whole town. Several people were going to Sorell for a function when they were suddenly taken up by Brady's gang and marched into town. The local constables and soldiers were settled in the lockup and homes were robbed.

Brady liked to give advance warning of attacks and issued a threat some time beforehand that he would raid the home of a local resident, Mr Richard Dry; but his threat was ignored. Obviously when news came to town that Mr Dry's home had, indeed, been raided the local commander, Colonel Balfour, rushed along with his troops. Then they got the idea that this was a decoy.

Rumours had spread far and wide that the Brady Gang was going to break into the Launceston Gaol and release all the prisoners before torturing and killing their former companion, the appalling Mark Jeffries. They did go into town, but robbed the home of another local identity, Mr Wedge, instead. The next day they robbed another property and burned the wheat stacks and barns, and the day after that they burned the house of a Mr Massey, after warning him that they would do so.

Brady was cheeky — well, he *was* an Irishman born in Manchester! He liked to act as the host in other people's expensive homes where the owners were forced to sit down with him at a dinner prepared from their own supplies by their own staff. When Colonel Balfour lost his hat during the Dry debacle Brady wore it in the next few raids, probably with a wide grin. But, as the stories of destruction show, although he didn't like pointless violence Brady was, deep down, a truly hard man.

He must have considered McCabe's love of the gun and the fist as pointless because he kicked him out of the gang. McCabe was captured and hanged shortly after, despite his best efforts to organise an independent life of crime.

It was probably their popularity as much as their actual crimes that so enraged Governor Arthur that he offered a reward of £25 for each member of the gang and hatched a plot.

One day the gang found a man named Cowan — a bolter — with some irons still attached. They took him in and found a blacksmith to remove the irons. Truth was Cowan had been allowed to escape on the understanding that, if he could trap Brady, he would receive a reward, a full pardon and a free trip home (which he got).

After being accepted by the gang, Cowan led them into several ambushes from which they escaped and he was fully involved in raids.

In the last battle many were killed on both sides and several bushrangers were captured. Brady was injured and limped off into the bush. He was tracked down by John Batman and his trackers and surrendered to Batman because he 'was not a soldier'.

Appeals, pleadings and tears could not save Brady from the hangman and he went to the gallows, either in the same batch as nine others or in one of the batches of two or three hanged on consecutive days in April 1826 (once again it all depends on which report you read). Whichever, some of those on the gallows were former members of his gang and one of those — which enraged Brady for being mixed up with such a one — was Jeffries.

Just a brief mention

There are many convict bushrangers that appear briefly in the records of an area of Tasmania, then they disappear. Britton and his gang are a small example of this lost group.

In October 1832 Britton (also known as Maurice Littleton) was one of a group who escaped from a number of assigned placements. One time when he was being recaptured he saved the life of a coastguard who had been thrown overboard during the inevitable struggle.

When he teamed up with George Jeffkins and Edward Brown he was accepted as leader. The brief records make it clear they had no qualms about firing first and asking second as they spent almost three years disrupting life in the northern part of the island. At one time people from Tamar were moving into Launceston, leaving almost all they owned behind them, to escape these three. It is recorded that Chief Constable

Cotterel captured Britton at Logans Falls on the North Esk River in 1834. He was tried, sentenced and reprieved, then he escaped from Hobart Town Hospital. He is supposed to have had a hiding place at Port Sorell where he was fed by servants from a property.

During a gunfight in 1835 Britton was wounded and eventually Jeffkins and Brown had to leave him while they searched for food. When they arrived near a hut at Port Sorell they were in bad shape. Brown was wearing a jacket in place of trousers and Jeffkin had blankets sewn around him. They tried to eat but were so far gone their stomachs couldn't hold anything down. Constables arrived and after another battle Brown was badly wounded and Jeffkins died.

As Brown died he said they had left Britton in a bad way and that he had probably died but other statements said it was not Britton who had been injured in the earlier fight. A report from one search party told of footprints found on a beach. The searchers agreed that the trail showed that one foot was bandaged and a brief report from Port Phillip in 1838 claimed that Britton had been captured and was being returned to Hobart Town.

James Dalton's bushranging career was one of the shortest, spanning from 28 December 1852 to April 1853.

Dalton was exceptionally tough: after arriving in Van Diemen's Land in March 1835 for his seven-year sentence he had eighteen months added within the first fortnight. He was flogged, set in the heaviest irons and put into solitary confinement. When he was sent to Norfolk Island as incurable in 1846, he immediately tried to bolt. Three years later he raped a young girl and had his sentence extended again. Then, in an about-face, he joined rescue services during the 1852 floods and received a four-month reduction in his sentence.

Back in Port Arthur he joined five other convicts in an escape by trying to swim past Eaglehawk Neck. Four drowned but Dalton and Andrew Kelly made it. Then they began bushranging. Within days they had robbed several houses and bailed up more than 30 people. When they attacked a watch-house keeper and two constables they killed the keeper, stole two thoroughbred horses and, in the next few weeks, raided several properties. On one occasion they held up a hut full of men and when one of them, a Constable Buckmaster, rushed at them he was shot by Dalton.

Easily recognised around Esk, they decided to go for the mainland. They tried to steal a schooner, then managed to take a whaleboat and forced four miners to take them across Bass Strait. They believed that if they reached Melbourne they could take a ship for England but they were too well known, as was the size of the reward offered for them — £500.

Dalton was conned into capture. He found a helpful boatman and they set out for a local coffee shop to exchange Tasmanian banknotes for gold. A customer named Brice said he was a gold broker and could make up the amount the shop could not fulfil. Brice had been a Melbourne police cadet and had a hunch about Dalton. He led him into the Police Court by the back door and challenged him as having stolen the banknotes. Dalton kept calm but then three detectives arrived and recognised him from his official description. Unable to use any of his three pistols Dalton conceded defeat and admitted, 'You have the reward of £500, my name is Dalton!'

Andrew Kelly was arrested the following day and they were both sent back to Tasmania. They were hanged on 26 April 1853 for the murder of Constable Buckmaster.

Cash & Co

The notorious Martin Cash must have been a romantic at heart because twice in his life it was love that brought him to account. The sentence that delivered him to New South Wales in 1827 was supposedly for attempted murder but the defence team claimed that he really shot the man because he (the man) was cuddling his (Cash's) girlfriend and cheery details about injuries to the man's buttocks were added to their plea.

Despite this heartrending tale Cash was sentenced and within a year he arrived in Sydney and was assigned to George Bowman in the Hunter Valley. Bowman must have been a good master because Cash stayed with him after being awarded a ticket-of-leave in 1834.

But three years later involvement in cattle duffing brought him to Van Diemen's Land, along with an army officer's wife, Bessie Clifford. His talent for being misunderstood hadn't deserted him and, though an early arrest brought no conviction, his attack on the arresting constables brought him the label of 'a marked man'. A later arrest did bring a conviction and he was sent to one of the convict settlements and attached to a work gang.

He escaped as quickly and as often as he could and during one of his free times he and Bessie decided to go to Melbourne. However, he was recaptured before they could travel and sent to the supposedly escape-proof Port Arthur by the ubiquitous John Price. A young officer assisting John Price said Price offered to treat Cash fairly if he behaved fairly. He escaped by swimming to the mainland but again was recaptured.

Two notorious bandits from New South Wales, Lawrence Kavanagh and George Jones, trusted the experienced Cash to find them a way out of gaol and he teamed up with them to make another run. After hiding in the bush for three days they swam the narrows but the clothes they had tried to carry on top of their heads were washed away. They struggled naked and barefoot through the bush, later described by Cash as laceratingly cruel, and were in a poor state when they came across a hut Cash remembered from an earlier escape and stole clothes and food.

After a few raids they hid out with a friend of Cash's while the wife went in to Hobart to bring Bessie back to join the group. After spending a few days chalking up more robberies, they set up a hideout on Mount Dromedary, 15 miles (24 kilometres) outside Hobart. They became known as 'Cash & Co' and acquired a reputation for good manners while robbing homesteads.

Some clothes and jewellery were stolen specifically for Bessie from a property at the foot of Mount Dromedary, and when she went to Hobart to avoid a determined search for the gang, she was arrested for being in possession of stolen goods. Cash wrote to Lieutenant-Governor Franklin demanding that this 'innocent lady of good name' be released and compensated or else the gang would administer a severe flogging to Franklin himself. Bessie was released, not out of fear of Cash, but in the hope that she would lead them to the gang.

When they pulled their first highway robbery on the Launceston passenger coach, two new trackers had arrived in Hobart and were on the trail straight away. In the inevitable gunfight that followed, Kavanagh was seriously injured when his gun exploded and he was forced to surrender.

Bessie hadn't returned to the gang after her release and Cash heard a rumour that she had gone along with another man. So, true to his nature, he set off to find her but was recognised in the street and had to make a run for it. He shot Constable Winstanley who confronted him, but was knocked out before he could get off any more shots.

Cash and Kavanagh were condemned to death for the constable's murder but Kavanagh was sent to Norfolk Island and Cash was kept in Hobart for fifteen months before being sent to Norfolk Island.

Cash himself seems to have quietened down during his ten years on Norfolk Island. His hostile relationship with John Price was revived there. Even so, he was considered responsible enough to have control of the boys' dormitories and in 1854 was given permission to marry Mary Bennett who was a convict servant in the house of the resident surgeon. Six months later as the second Norfolk Island settlement was closing down he received a ticket-of-leave. Upon his release Cash and his wife moved to Tasmania and stayed for a while, where Cash cared for the municipal gardens in Hobart. Their son was born in 1855 and Cash spent some time in New Zealand from 1856. He covers this period in a short sentence in his memoir but a report from New Zealand gives more information.

According to this record he joined the Canterbury Province Armed Police Force in 1859. His reason for doing this was, apparently, to get an inside line on police actions to protect his main business — running a brothel. Some of his colleagues began to doubt him and his background was checked more thoroughly. Inevitably, he was sacked when the results came in and was later fined for keeping a brothel. After he returned to Tasmania, the family settled on a property in Glenorchy. He died there in 1871 from rheumatic fever.

Jones, who had managed to escape, tried to set up another gang including men like Dalton and Liddell (who asked for death before Norfolk Island when they were tried), but was blinded by a shotgun blast during a gun battle and was hanged six months later.

Jackey Jackey is moved on again

By September 1845 William Westwood (Jackey Jackey) had been in Port Arthur for over three years. He had made a run for it twice in the first year and was ordered 100 lashes. During his third escape he swam across the channel while his companions were taken by sharks. In November 1843 he got twelve months with hard labour — three of the months in solitary confinement.

The following year the new commandant, W T Champ, promoted Westwood to his boat crew and, after his courage in the rescue of two men, Westwood was allowed to serve six months' probation at Glenorchy along the Derwent River. Four months later he was on trial in the Hobart Supreme Court for robbery, but because he had not injured anyone, his death sentence was changed to life on Norfolk Island.

Norfolk Island was a harsh place waiting to blow up. Despite the cold desires of the administrators, one, a Captain Maconochie, eased conditions — just a little — and convicts were allowed to grow their own vegetables and own their eating irons and billies. A new commandant, Major Joseph Childs, was ordered to return to firmness and the cutlery and the billies were removed.

The next morning, 1 July 1846, as warders went around calling prisoners to get up, William Westwood finally blew up and attacked a warder, knocking him down. Other warders came in to rescue their mate and eventually Westwood killed an overseer and several constables. Other prisoners joined the attack and many were injured as order was restored and the mutiny was put down with the brutality of desperation.

Twenty-six men were charged with mutiny and twelve, including Westwood, were hanged on 13 October 1846. Another of those hanged was Martin Cash's mate Lawrence

Kavanagh. When Martin Cash told his life story to Lester Burke, many years later, he stressed the point that Kavanagh was out in the yard at the time of the mutiny and could not have been in any way involved. But one story claims that Kavanagh broke down the door of the room where the billies and cutlery had been stored.

The young in care

Across the bay from Port Arthur is a narrow spit of land, next door to the Isle of the Dead. This patch of land was named Point Puer after *puer*, the Latin word for 'boy', and there was a juvenile penal station there from 1834 to 1849 for boys with the average age of fifteen. In a report by Lieutenant-Governor Charles La Trobe, he noted that the boys were well supplied with books and maps in their school and that the trades were reasonably well taught. These trades included boot making, carpentry and baking. Access to the station by adults was strictly supervised.

Many of the better-known convicts started their lives in Australia here. William Westwood (Jackey Jackey) was sixteen, Edward Davis of the Jewboy Gang was seventeen, Boyd of the Rammer Gang was approximately fourteen, and Captain Melville was transported at the age of thirteen.

One very young inmate was Rares. He was transported at the age of nine for a minimal offence — supposedly stealing an apple. By the time he was sixteen he was hardened and managed to sneak across Point Puer and escaped. He made his way to Hobart Town and then to New Norfolk. There he walked into a police station and stole weapons and money. After that he travelled towards Launceston and met up with two bushrangers named Lawton and Cowden.

During an attack on a house at South Esk River, Lawton took a shot to the mouth and lost his teeth and part of his tongue. Rares was on the roof and when he fired down to the street the gun exploded blowing off his right hand. A Mr Thompson did what he could for him then took him by cart to Launceston Gaol. The wound was cauterised with a hot iron to stop the bleeding but Rares was probably too far gone to notice much in his last week of life. When it came time to examine him he was considered 'too near death to say a word' and was hanged the following morning.

Another young inmate was Henry Bradley. Henry was eleven when he was orphaned and was brought up by a gang of pickpockets. He must have been quite young when caught because he was sent straight to Point Puer. As an adult (approximately 22 years of age) he was assigned to a Mr McKay and, along with his friend Patrick O'Connor who was in service with Mr Gibson, he bolted. They had six weeks of freedom and crime before they were hanged.

The two men attacked with double-barrelled shotguns and tied people up. When one man escaped they shot his companion in revenge. Then they moved on to a nearby farm where they forced the farmer's wife to cook breakfast for them. After breakfast they crossed the river to another property, stole another gun and some food and planned their escape to the mainland.

After forcing the crew of the *Sophia* to take them across Bass Strait, they coerced two crewmen to row them to shore. Neither the crewmen nor the rowboat were ever seen again.

From there they moved on to Brighton, looking for some horses to steal. They came to a farm, and on hearing that all the horses were being used for ploughing, they ordered a ploughman to unhitch a couple. When the ploughman thought it was a joke they shot him.

They hit two more stations after that. At the first one they killed a gardener who tried to help the owner; at the second they bailed up eleven men and ransacked the place. By now the police had caught up with them. They escaped briefly but the police caught up again and they were captured.

They were hanged in October 1853.

Chapter 4

THE DISTRICT, THE BAY AND THE SWAN

The 'bookends' of New South Wales would eventually become their own independent states: the Port Phillip District would be known as Victoria after 1850 and the northern district — Moreton Bay — would be officially declared Queensland in 1855. However, before then they had their convicts and their troubles.

The Port Phillip District

Joseph Dignum and George Comerford were probably the first bushrangers in the district. Dignum had been one of three convicts who bolted from Yass in 1837. They were later joined by another group of six, one of whom was Comerford. With Dignum in charge of the gang, they spent a little time attracting the rage of the seven police officers who covered the Yass region, with raids on isolated homes. Even with such limited official resources, they eventually felt the region had become overexploited and decided to move south, but the group ran out of provisions and quarrelled about exactly where to go.

Dignum and Comerford decided to split from the group and one night, near Mount Alexander, they waited for the others to go to sleep. With axes in hand they crept up on their companions, but something disturbed at least one of the men and only four were initially killed. The remaining three had to be shot or further battered before all the bodies could be thrown onto a fire which had been lit to cremate the bodies.

Because they were short of food Dignum and Comerford backtracked and found a job with a squatter for a while. They broke their contract and moved to another property and the original squatter chased up their work agreement and had them arrested. Before the case came to court they bolted again, but Dignum decided that his intended trip to the hopeful new settlement of South Australia should be taken alone. His attempt to shoot Comerford didn't work out and Comerford decided to go to Melbourne and turn his old mate in.

Both men were taken to Sydney for trial because there was no appropriate court available in Melbourne. In one of his statements Comerford told the authorities about the Mount Alexander massacre. When no one would believe it possible, the authorities escorted Comerford back to the site to check out his story. There they found the charred bones and clothing.

During the journey back to Melbourne, Comerford constantly complained about having to walk in handcuffs, so they released him during the day. During one day's trek the officers realised they had left their tea and sugar behind at the previous night's campsite and two of the officers were sent back to collect them. The remaining officer, Sergeant Tomkins, continued to leave his weapon propped against a tree and to leave Comerford unsecured. When Comerford made a run for the gun the sergeant made a run for Comerford and died the minute his unsecured prisoner pulled the trigger.

Comerford went back to his old ground and a reward of £50 was offered for his capture. He was recognised immediately when he wandered into a bush hut and, as he stood casually lighting his pipe, the occupant knocked him out and handed him in.

Comerford was taken back to Melbourne and was tried and hanged for the murder of Sergeant Tomkins. Dignum got life on Norfolk Island where he was hanged some years later for the murder of a police sergeant during an escape attempt.

Captain Melville has arrived

Francis McCallum — better known as Captain Melville — was born in Scotland in 1823. When he was arrested for housebreaking at the age of thirteen, he already had a criminal record and was sent to Point Puer in Van Diemen's Land, arriving in 1838. McCallum was undisciplined and given to bouts of uncontrollable fury. Almost immediately he received twenty lashes for his bad behaviour and another 36 for repeated insolence.

Between 1839 and 1848 he was before the magistrates a staggering 25 times and his punishments included regular 36 lashes and long periods of hard labour, sometimes in chains. He still managed to bolt three times: in November 1848, January 1850 and April 1850. This last time he got clear and late in 1851 he began to make his name in Victoria.

When Frank McCallum arrived in Victoria in 1851, he swung through the Mount Macedon and Geelong areas, robbing travellers and stealing horses. He was supposedly holding up travellers along the western track across the Wimmera from the central goldfields: the police claimed they had almost captured him at Mount Arapiles; a carter and his sons described him and two companions who attacked them on Fiery Creek Plains as having faces like hawks. Many of the actions tied to him may have been those of other men called Melville or McCallum, or just about anybody.

In 1852 he met up with another well-known villain called William Roberts. Their most notorious deed took place at a property run by a Mr Aitcheson. The two of them alone tied up eighteen men and ordered a meal be prepared by Mrs Aitcheson. After the meal they went through the home and the property taking whatever they fancied and collecting two horses as they left, promising the men tied up in the barn that they would be released by Mrs Aitcheson shortly.

Melville was lucky enough to escape attempts to capture him and the reward of £100 for his capture, dead or alive, was never sought — perhaps his reputation for ungovernable rage meant no one got close enough to try. Still, he and Roberts continued their raids and around Christmas 1852 they made enough money from other Christmas travellers to decide they had earned a celebration. They rode into Geelong and had a good dinner and bought some brandy before moving on to a brothel. Melville got drunk enough to tell everyone who he was and boasted of his exploits. One of the women ran for the police, probably with an eye to the reward, but Melville began to sense danger and tried to drag the totally incapable Roberts along with him. He couldn't move his mate so he ran out the front door alone in time to see two constables just reaching the steps. He ran back through the house and out the back door where he knocked down a third officer. Chased down the street by several more officers, he ran into a fellow named Mr Guy. He pulled Mr Guy off his horse and tried to make his escape, but the horse was going home to stables and wasn't having any stranger on his back. Captain Melville was thrown and grabbed by Mr Guy who hung on to him until the officers arrived.

In February 1853 Roberts got twelve years, while Melville was sentenced to 32 years and taken to the hulk *President*, which sat in Hobsons Bay. (By now the district was swamped with gold seekers, including many former convicts. The old routine of turning useless ships into overnight lockups was considered the only answer to the growing number of lawbreakers.) Melville was still subject to violent moods and always in trouble. Late in 1856, while he and some other prisoners were being transferred between the hulks, they seized a boat. Somebody bashed and killed Corporal Owen and Melville was seen waving a hammer during the brief escape. Picked up by the water police, he was sentenced to hang, but was eventually given life in Melbourne Gaol. He was supposedly heard to say, 'You'll be sorry for it' when told of the new sentence.

His mood swings became more common and he attacked the governor of the gaol. His rages were increasingly violent and he was placed under medical supervision. The staff was warned to stay away from him during an attack.

At this time John Price, formerly of Norfolk Island, was Inspector-General of Victoria's prisons, despite his initial objection to the idea. When he went to talk to the convicts at Williamstown about their conditions, a stone flew through the air and the prisoners charged. Price was injured and later died in hospital. Although Melville had been removed from the quarry before the event, he was accused of having organised and planned this attempt at mutiny.

In August 1857, after another violent episode, Melville, who was probably in his mid-thirties by now, was found in his cell with a large handkerchief tied around his neck. If suicide was one verdict, another was that he was no great loss and everyone was the better without him.

The gold ship

I suppose the attack on the *Nelson* could be considered a form of piracy, but as the ship was still being loaded and the perpetrators were mainly bolters, it will fit into this story.

In April 1852 the *Nelson* was waiting in Hobsons Bay for

the rest of her cargo en route to London. The most famous part of her cargo had already been loaded: 8000 ounces of gold, packed in 23 boxes and valued at, then, £25,000. There was no secrecy about this and three visitors to Melbourne came up with a brilliant plan — they would steal the gold.

These three men — John James (also known as Johnston), James Morgan and James Duncan — had varied records. Morgan was a bolter from Van Diemen's Land (arriving in the district some time between 1829 and 1836) and his real name was James Gavagan. In 1845 he was given another fifteen years in a Melbourne court and sent back to Van Diemen's Land but absconded again and returned to Melbourne.

John James had several records including the names of the ships he had arrived on and the sentences he had received. However, early in 1852, he was living in the region.

James Duncan came from London and claimed to be a free traveller, but in the early 1850s he was living in the Keilor Plains in the Black Forest region and was studying bushranging along with James and Morgan. The three decided they needed some help on this big job and recruited Stephen Fox, William Barnes, Edward Wilson and Dan Fagan (who had contacts on the ship and was able to slip aboard to reconnoitre a few days earlier).

On the night of 2 April 1852, they stole two boats from the owner of a hotel near the *Nelson*'s anchorage and rowed across to the loot. There were few people on board and all were asleep. The gang rounded them up and ordered the mate, Mr Draper, to lead them to the gold. He refused and was shot in the side, with the promise of more to come. He led them to the store where they broke off the door and collected the boxes of gold before herding their prisoners into the store and nailing the broken door back in place.

When the stevedores arrived the next day they released the prisoners and the hunt was on. A reward of £750 was offered for their capture and the trio were soon arrested. They went to trial on 28 May 1852 and all received fifteen years on a road gang with the first three years ordered to be spent in irons.

James went to the hulk *President* and was still in irons at the end of December 1856. In June 1858 he received a free pardon and was released.

Morgan spent time in Melbourne Gaol and, when on the hulks, was a devoted maker of trouble and receiver of punishments. In November 1860, he received a ticket-of-leave for the district of Melbourne.

Duncan had got as far as Williamstown before being picked up and was also a troublesome prisoner. Late in 1858 he seems to have calmed down and in March 1860 he got his ticket-of-leave to the Keilor district. After five years he was in court again, charged with 'burglary and stealing', and received four years' hard labour. Still misbehaving, he was released in February 1870 but was back in gaol with a ten-year sentence by May 1870, again for theft. Behaving quite well during his last sentence, he died on December 1875 — his death recorded as being the result of an 'abscess on the liver'.

Fagan is listed in some records as being the leader of a group who escaped from the 'sister island' and returned to Melbourne, then was sent back to Van Diemen's Land before eventually (according to the *Yass Courier* October 1867) trying his luck in Queensland and disappearing.

Another Melville

Another Melville — George 'Frenchy' Melville — carried out the first so-called 'biggest' gold robbery in Australia. Melville, together with a large gang of bushrangers, including William

Atkins, George Wilson, John and Joseph Francis, Ned McIvoy, Joe Grey, Bob Harding, George Elson and a man named 'Billy', carried out the robbery.

In July 1853 the Melbourne Gold Escort Company was planning to move 2223 ounces of gold and £700 in notes and coins to Melbourne from the McIvor diggings. The dray carrying the loot was to meet up with a government gold escort at Kyneton, and when the driver, Thomas Flookes, set off with his horses he had four companions: the boss, two other company employees and a police sergeant.

Twenty miles into their journey, the road was blocked by a fallen log. Flookes was easing his team around the log when shots from a nearby shelter fatally wounded him and his companions turned around and ran. The dray was now in the hands of George Melville and his friends.

There had been other such robberies but this was the biggest thus far and a massive manhunt was organised. John Francis and George Wilson, plus their wives, were found aboard the *Madagascar* in Hobsons Bay and were arrested. Melville and his wife were picked up on the *Callooney*, while Mr and Mrs Atkins had bought tickets for the *Hellespont* but were picked up in a boarding house.

Apparently there are no documents relating to the case left so information is patchy. Joseph Francis may have been arrested in Queensland then released after informing, but another report says he was picked up by a police cadet on the Campaspe River, and committed suicide on the way back to Melbourne.

Seven bags of gold and some coins and bank notes were recovered, but the rest of the gold disappeared along with the remaining five or six thieves.

Melville, Atkins and Wilson were charged with the murder of Flookes and hanged in October 1853. As usual, there was a large crowd to witness the hangings and the bodies were handed over to their families as soon as they were cut down. Melville's wife took his body back to be displayed in the window of an oyster shop in Bourke Street as an advertising gimmick. As a result, the authorities ordered that, in future, the bodies of the hanged would be buried in prison grounds.

Not all great planners

Not every bushranger well known in his time is recorded and not all their actions make sense. Henry Garrett's name was recognised in Victorian bushranging circles during 1854, which makes it difficult to understand why he and three other men — Thomas Quinn, Henry Merriott and John Boulton — robbed the Bank of Victoria in Ballarat with unloaded guns. However, they were successful and Garrett got away to England. He was arrested there and returned to Victoria and sentenced to ten years. During his sentencing the judge, Redmond Barry (who would later sentence Ned Kelly amongst others), declared that although the sentences 'might be considered harsh ... they will be mitigated as the country becomes more settled and composed'.

After receiving a ticket-of-leave in 1861, Garrett left for New Zealand where, according to the Melbourne *Argus* he was inspired by the beautiful countryside to 'rob 23 persons in one day'. He got eight years' penal servitude in Dunedin Gaol. On release he got a job in Otago but the local police commissioner had him sent back to Melbourne, where they didn't want him. The Melbourne authorities also told him to move on, but where he moved on to doesn't seem to be recorded.

The cruel, hot bay

The Moreton Bay convicts were listed under the general New South Wales category until 1842, when the New South Wales government cancelled the bay's status as a penal settlement but, until that point, it was another place designated as a convict colony and it was described as a very rough and ready place. This rough and readiness included an army store along with barracks for the soldiers and convicts and a few tents and bark huts. For work there was a sawpit, a brick kiln and a blacksmith's shop. It had settled into a small colony of approximately 100 people by the end of 1825, ready for its reputation as the worst place a convicted person could be sent to, and those who were sent there, were condemned to be 'properly ironed'.

The camp commandant up until 1829 was Captain Patrick Logan, not only a very efficient man but also very tough and very unyielding in his authority, although he is recorded as not approving of corporal punishment but being unable to avoid it in his early days in the settlement. What had become Brisbane Town grew quickly, with its convict population reaching 1020 by 1831, and it may have missed his firm command when he was murdered in October 1830 during an exploratory trip to the Brisbane River headwaters.

Although disturbances and fighting were common in Logan's time, in response to his stern discipline, it must have been even tougher under his successor, Captain James Clunie, whose list of punishments includes 250 lashes for a fourth absconding and 300 for a seventh attempt.

Moreton Bay was particularly difficult for convicts and settlers alike. This was the first time most of them had ever spent time in a sub-tropical climate. The drought of 1828–29 and the crop failure in 1828 resulted in the same short rations seen in the early days of Port Jackson. Despite the shortages, 126 prisoners bolted with flour, fat and corn they had stolen from the public stores. Eventually 69 returned to the settlement hungry and exhausted, where they received up to 300 lashes and had three years added to their sentences. Potential escapers were afraid of the local Aborigines and none were recorded as making it fully away from the bay; under Clunie's regime fewer tried. Anyone who did make it went north because China was in that direction.

One who took the chance was John Graham. Transported in 1824 for theft of hempen rope he was originally assigned in Parramatta where he was friendly with the local Aborigines and learned some bush skills from them. Charged and convicted again he was transported to Moreton Bay and bolted. Local Aboriginal people believed he was the spirit of a dead warrior and accepted his presence in the tribe where he stayed for six years before returning to Moreton Bay and presenting himself to a disbelieving Clunie. Graham played the 'imprisoned by savages' card to try and buy himself a friendly reception and a pardon as a noble sufferer. This didn't work but in 1837 he got his ticket-of-leave and a start-up bonus of £10.

Along the Swan

In 1827 a small party of soldiers and convicts was sent to establish a British presence in what was to become Western Australia. But in 1829 Western Australia set itself out to be a *free* colony; 'no convicts' was the aim, in part because of the horror stories everyone had heard from the eastern colonies.

People who had the capital for development under government control were granted land in the new colony. Mostly such settlers didn't fancy the labouring life; they aimed for a gentry one — and the wage-rate of hard work came high.

Eventually the settlers asked for cheap labour and convicts were dispatched at speed; such speed that when, in 1850, the *Scindian* arrived with 75 convicts, she had to sit offshore for two months because no one knew where to put them.

By the end of the convict era, Western Australia had received 9720 convicts on 43 ships, but they came from and arrived in very different worlds to those recorded earlier. Maybe this is why there are so few records of bolters and bushrangers in Western Australia. Another point is that with a busy port such as Bunbury, where ships were loading goods and horses for eager overseas markets and where American whaler crews might have been sympathetic to escaped convicts, there were pleasanter alternatives to the roving life for any bolter. But one who did attract attention was 'bad' in a different way. He was a nuisance of the first order as far as the authorities were concerned and, perhaps, in this way he became the real 'ideal' bushranger as romanticised by some in the east.

Welsh-born Joseph Bolitho Johns, who became known as Moondyne Joe, arrived as Convict Number 1790 on the *Pyrenees* in 1853. His crimes were fairly minor and as a reward for his good behaviour, he was given a ticket-of-leave on arrival. In March 1855, he received a conditional pardon and he was able to leave town and travel around the bush doing various jobs. Moondyne Joe had a way with horses and as well as breaking them in he could find the occasional wanderers and earn a little extra money by returning them to their owners. In August 1861 there was one horse he found that was recorded as an unbranded cleanskin so Joe branded it for himself. This led to his arrest after some spiteful rumours said he was so good at finding horses because he stole them in the first place for the sake of the rewards. Gaoled, he (according to which source you read) either removed the screws holding up the cell door and collected the newly branded horse from the station yard and left, or he used a fork to scratch away the mortar between a couple of stone blocks in the cell wall then slipped through the hole and hid in the hay loft while the police searched for him in the surrounding bush.

Whichever plan, it only worked for a while and when recaptured in the Moondyne Hills he was sentenced to three years for escaping from custody, as there was no evidence for a charge of horse stealing. He served his time peacefully and was released in February 1864. He found work on a farm in Kelmscott but, in January 1865, he was accused of killing and eating a neighbour's steer and was sentenced to ten years' penal servitude, all the while protesting his innocence. As he felt this unjust, he escaped again, determined not to pay for a crime he did not commit. It is now that he earned the name 'Moondyne Joe'. Captured, again, he was put in irons and locked in a cell. When a warder looked in on him he was well on the way to cutting the lock out of the cell door. Recorded as a troublesome prisoner he was decorated with stronger irons — but escaped again within a fortnight.

After cutting off his irons he hooked up with three other escapees and together they committed various robberies around Perth, narrowly escaping capture numerous times. Realising that he could not elude the police forever, he planned to travel to the new colony of South Australia. For this plan to work he would need food and equipment. On 5 September he robbed the Toodyay store and then started travelling east, but was eventually captured when police discovered his tracks.

Now officially a 'runaway', he wore the black and yellow bolter suit and an extra set of chains, along with the celebrity status of successful bad boy. He had escaped from every situation the authorities had placed him in and new arrivals from England were entertained with tales of his exploits. His boast that no chains, special cells or guards could keep him captive infuriated unpopular Governor John Hampton and his equally unpopular comptroller-general son. They declared that *they* could keep Moondyne Joe and commissioned a very special escape-proof cell to house him.

This special cell was a cage built on the third floor of the Convict Establishment at Fremantle. The jarrah walls were studded with dog collar spikes, the window was double barred and it had a hole-studded steel plate nailed across it. Joe was locked in this cage, still wearing chains, and fed on bread and water.

After some months the prison doctor insisted that Joe must have fresh air and exercise if they wanted to keep him alive, so a job was devised.

Every day, after the prison gangs left for their work, Joe was taken down to the yard where a mound of stones was set for breaking. One guard spent the whole day, every day, watching Joe break stones and build a pile of rubble. The plan was to clear this debris every day, but it never was, and the finished heap grew higher and higher. The bored guard could no longer see Joe but he could hear the rhythmic hammer blows and would call out and Joe would answer. One day all was quiet and Joe didn't answer, but the guard could see his hat and parts of his gaudy uniform behind the rock pile and kindly left him to have an innocent nap. But Joe was gone! Behind the mound of broken rocks he had dug his way through the yard wall into the garden of the superintendent's house. There he marched out the gate wearing his long underwear and boots — his uniform being worn by the rake and hammer in the yard.

Alarms were rung and searches began. Children in the street sang a popular ditty about the governor, to the tune of 'Pop Goes the Weasel':

The Governor's son has got the pip,
The Governor's got the measles.
For Moondyne Joe has give 'em the slip,
Pop goes the weasel.

They couldn't keep him after all.

It was two years before he was seen again and then it was just bad luck. Mr Ferguson, a local vineyard owner, and some troopers, had been searching for the body of a worker who had drowned in the nearby river. They came back from the search wet and cold and Mr Ferguson went down to his cellar to bring out a few warming jugs of wine. He lit his small candle and was moving between rows of barrels when a wild yell introduced a weird figure springing from the shadows behind one of the rows. Joe! He wore a wheat sack, with a hole cut out for his head. His hair was wild around his shoulders and his long beard covered his chest. He had tied sheepskins over his boots to hide his tracks and his feet made no sound as he turned to run but the troopers rushed into the cellar in response to the yell and Joe was back in custody.

This was February 1869, a year after the end of transportation in Western Australia. Maybe that is why Joe settled down to serve out his sentence before being granted a ticket-of-leave in 1871 and moving to the Vasse district to work as a timber cutter. A pleasant and popular man, he married and lived in the Toodyay region. Joseph Bolitho Johns was 22 years of age when he arrived in Western Australia in 1853 and, despite his adventures and tough times, he lived a full life and died at the age of 89.

Chapter 5

DEEDS AND WORDS

Bushrangers are only part of this new world: everyone involved contributed in some way, large or small, and here we look at just a few members of two groups who did: the women and the authorities.

The ladies ... bless 'em

Most of the women transported as convicts were first-time prisoners. They believe that one in every five convicts on the First Fleet was a female who came from England or Ireland. Most of them were sentenced for a fairly minor crime such as pickpocketing or shoplifting.

Of the women mentioned as convicts, most eventually beat the system and made good in a man's world. People like Mary Reibey and Esther Graham, whose names are well known, stand out as exceptional, but there must have been many more who just got on with life.

Mary Bryant is a well-known name for quite another reason. Cornish-born (1765) into a family of well-known sheep thieves, Mary was sentenced in 1786 for assault and robbery and, initially, was sentenced to death. Eventually her sentence was reduced to 'a seven' and she was transported in the *Charlotte*. During the voyage she gave birth to a baby, described as a 'fine girl'. In February 1788, Mary married William Bryant, who was also Cornish. Bryant, a smuggler, was originally sentenced to the Americas but was re-routed via the *Charlotte*, where he was responsible for issuing prisoner rations.

Settled in Port Jackson, Bryant was able to start a small vegetable garden and was supposedly in charge of fishing boats. Unfortunately, he sold some of the fish independently and was sentenced to 100 lashes, although his fishing skills were still valued. Emmanuel, Mary's second child, was born in April 1790 and later that year a Dutch ship, the *Waaksamheyd* arrived with much needed provisions. Bryant was able to source weapons and food, along with sea-going needs such as a chart, a compass and a quadrant, from the ship's master, Captain Smit.

Known to have escape in mind, Bryant was watched, but in March 1791, with no ship available for pursuit, the Bryants and seven other convicts escaped in the governor's cutter. The vessel had been newly provisioned and serviced with new masts and sails but, even so, the journey to Timor was dangerous. Their voyage was an exploration as well as an escape and during their 69 days at sea they discovered coal along the coast and recorded uncharted islands along the Great Barrier Reef before reaching Koepang early in June. There they claimed to be survivors from a shipwreck but the authorities learned the truth and they were imprisoned.

When the survivors of the *Pandora*, along with the *Bounty* prisoners, arrived at Koepang in September, the captain, Edward Edwards, had more to worry about than escaped convicts and he did not take them into his custody until October. They travelled in chains and after they arrived in Batavia in December little Emmanuel died, three weeks before his father William.

During the voyage from South Africa to England, Mary's young daughter Charlotte died, just five weeks before they reached their destination.

The case of Mary and the other convicts attracted a massive press reaction and a mysterious person (later discovered to be the biographer James Boswell) provided financial support for Mary after her return to Cornwall. He led the appeal for clemency and Mary was pardoned six weeks after her original sentence had expired. A letter thanking Boswell for a gift was the last heard of Mary — a bolter of distinction.

In the early days of settlement all convict women lived as the male convicts did, except in separate quarters, and were generally assigned as domestics to military families or settlers, but in 1804 the female factories were established. Work was allocated in three categories: spinning and carding with some money from profits to be paid to the women (this was the top level and the women had to 'work their way up'); the next group did similar work but had less status and no money; while the third group did hard labour such as moving earth and breaking stones and were given no tea or sugar. Even public complaints about the lack of tea and sugar didn't ease things for this class of prisoner. Other female factories were built in Ross and the Cascades in Van Diemen's Land and at Moreton Bay (now in southern Queensland). The factory at Ross housed troublesome and hardened female prisoners and pregnant convicts awaiting assignment. Free settlers would come to the factories and seek female labour or prospective wives. When the earlier disorderly society settled, many women were married from the female factories and moved into a more regular life.

Although the records don't tell of female bolters or bushrangers, some stories of bail-ups and raids often mention

Aboriginal girls holding horses or pointing shotguns at the bewildered travellers and most of the regular groups must have had female companionship at times, but there are few names recorded.

Then there were the women recorded in the bushranger tales. Bessie Clifford doesn't seem to been an active participant in Martin Cash's escapades, and when he married some years after losing her to another man, he wed a convict with an ordinary job and lived, in part, the kind of ordinary life she could provide.

One source refers to a girl dressed as a man being seen with the Britton gang and there may well have been more.

Mary Cockerill, Michael Howe's companion, may have been more involved — if only in fanciful reporting. It was probably an accident when he shot her as they were making a run for it, but she didn't forgive him and passed on all the information she could to the authorities. One report says she died in hospital, but it doesn't seem to be as the result of Michael's bullet.

The gentlemen who made the rules

So many of the names mentioned in this book are career public officials. From the army, navy or a fairly high level of society, they played their part in developing this country. People like governors Phillip, Hunter, Darling, Franklin, Arthur, Hampton, and King did their duty according to their individual standards and abilities. People like Maconochie tried to make changes and got little in return.

Official names appear in the convict world; some close at hand and some on the other side of the globe. Many who made the decisions about what would happen in this new land showed no interest in those who would be living out the results of those decisions and, judging by some of the orders and the planning involved, those decisions were made by people who not only knew nothing, but were unwilling to learn.

We can look closely at some of the people literally on the front-line in the new colony and at the responsibilities involved as well as the records of their governing styles and the results of those styles.

Captain Alexander Maconochie was a man of theories and beliefs. His views on the care and treatment of prisoners were to be tried out on Norfolk Island after Sir John Franklin replaced the severe disciplinarian Sir George Arthur as lieutenant-governor of Tasmania in 1836. Maconochie, along with his wife, six children and a new group of convicts, arrived on Norfolk Island in March 1840. His efforts did not receive support from Governor Gipps in Sydney and including convicts in the Queen's birthday celebrations outraged disciplinarians (seen specifically as an 'English' event, rarely a Scottish one and never an Irish one according to Gipps), while concerns about specific unnatural offences eventually provided the excuse for Maconochie's replacement.

Norfolk's tyrants

Joseph Childs, who initially replaced Maconochie, was a weak man and an inexperienced administrator who wanted to be everybody's friend but who, when pushed, overreacted so that, inevitably, his administration was a failure. Both Comptroller-General of convicts Colonel Champ and Childs' replacement John Price believed that Childs' ineptitude and his spiteful attempts to amend the situation by removing the only things the convicts actually owned (thereby creating a response he would probably never understand) were responsible for the violent attacks by convicts upon warders on 1 July 1846. Childs left the island in August 1846 and returned to England where he received several promotions and lived to a grand old age.

John Price's name comes up in different places and he was certainly efficient. He took up farming in the Huon River district of Van Diemen's Land and was eventually a stipendiary magistrate and controller of convicts. Considered a tough administrator, some of the punishments he meted out were savage. His replacement of the inept Childs was just in time to organise the trials of the 26 men accused of involvement in the so-called mutiny, but it was badly timed for Price himself who was supposed to be on sick leave on a doctor's recommendation.

He stifled all disagreement and ordered the Anglican chaplain, Reverend Thomas Rogers, off the island after Rogers made several complaints about his abuse of power and cruelty, and evidence from the Catholic bishop of Van Diemen's Land seems to confirm his tyrannical attitudes there; but he offered fair dealings to Martin Cash in exchange for fair dealings in return.

When Price was appointed Inspector-General of Victoria in 1854, he didn't want to go but he finally accepted the position. His reputation travelled with him and investigations began in 1856 into the appalling conditions under his administration. It would be dishonest not to concede that many of these conditions resulted from the massive increase in lawlessness and the need for the hulks. Price gave evidence but died before the enquiry concluded. On 26 March 1857, he visited Williamstown to investigate complaints made by convicts about the rations meted out to them. Here an angry mob of convicts attacked him and the next day he died from the injuries. Bushranger Captain Melville was blamed for organising the attack, although he had been moved from the area some time before the event.

Charles La Trobe

Charles Joseph La Trobe's father, Christian, was a missionary and, like him, Charles was an anti-slavery speaker who had dealings with noted anti-slavery campaigner William Wilberforce. La Trobe wrote books about climbing and mountain life and about his travels in America with the American author Washington Irving. Sent to report on slaves in the West Indies, he wrote poetry while there, before returning to England where he was appointed Superintendent of the Port Phillip District, which was still part of New South Wales. He arrived in Melbourne on 30 September 1839 with his wife and daughter, two servants and a prefabricated house.

With no military or naval background, La Trobe was different to other colonial administrators. He was a typical educated gentleman of the era, keen to learn new things and add to learning overall. As superintendent, all his decisions had to be approved by the governor in Sydney. When the separationist movement got under way (a body calling for Victoria to become a new, independent colony), La Trobe agreed that it would be the best thing that could happen and he disapproved of sending convicts there. Indeed, when in 1849, he refused to let the *Randolph* land its convict cargo at Port Philip and ordered the ship on to Sydney, he was directly disobeying Colonial Office instructions.

Although regularly criticised by advocates for separation for not pushing the cause or the needs of Port Phillip strongly enough, La Trobe governed in one of the most difficult periods in terms of severe depression and a land boom burst. Acting as Lieutenant-Governor of Van Diemen's Land for four months between 1846 and 1847, he prepared a report for Earl Grey about the state of convicts and their prospects, which is a major resource for students of the era and the system.

When the *Australian Colonies Government Act* of 1850 declared Victoria an independent entity, La Trobe became Lieutenant-Governor with an Executive Council of four. When he wanted to replace the diggers' mining licence with a gold export levy, the council refused to agree and were responsible for much of the trouble that followed.

By the middle of 1852, La Trobe had established government control, although his hands were full maintaining order. Roads and wharves needed to be built and no provisions had been made for the thousands of immigrants and ships arriving from overseas. La Trobe may have underestimated the magnitude of the gold discoveries and the number of prospectors it would bring, and the Legislative Council was unhelpful when he tried to calm gold field temper by changing the method of taxation. He eventually began to reserve land for future sale in pastoral areas and allowed squatters to buy homestead blocks, but his delay in bringing small sections of land for sale near the gold fields aroused hostility from gold diggers, who also objected to the high cost of these blocks.

La Trobe resigned in 1852 but was not relieved until 1854. His wife had already returned to England because of ill health and had died before he could join her. He died in 1875 in Sussex, England.

Administration in Van Diemen's Land

Lieutenant-Colonel Thomas Davey was a royal marine who had travelled on the First Fleet as a volunteer guard. He returned to England but was later appointed as Lieutenant-Governor of Van Diemen's Land. When he arrived in Sydney in October 1812 he had no luggage — that had travelled on a ship attacked by American privateers.

While waiting in Sydney to travel on to his post in Van Diemen's Land, Davey convinced Governor Macquarie that he was a buffoon and a frivolous idiot. Davey proved Macquarie right as a poor manager of money who ran up huge debts and Macquarie felt impelled to oversee Davey's observance of the rules, insisting that Davey was not to draw bills on the British Treasury nor to charter ships, grant lands or make any contracts without the governor's permission. Macquarie lost no time in advising the British government to remove him.

Having no criminal court in Hobart, Davey had no means of trying bushrangers and declared martial law in April 1815, even though this was illegal. Macquarie refused to take any responsibility for Davey's actions, but allowed the situation to continue for six months.

Although he seems not to have been a very bright man, Davey does seem to have been able to attract benefits to himself. His regime did progress despite the poor resources allocated. A gaol and church were built, the ports of Hobart and Dalrymple were opened to trade, and some police reforms were instigated during his time in office.

Macquarie's advice was finally accepted and, in April 1816, Davey was removed from his post, to be replaced by William Sorell. Davey went to Sydney demanding compensation for losses during his post and was granted 8000 acres (3238 hectares) of land. He returned to Hobart in June 1818 as a settler. He died in London on 2 May 1823, while trying to settle some private affairs in England.

William Sorell was born in 1775 and, as the son of a senior army officer, he took up his own commission. He was involved in several fairly minor actions before becoming Deputy Adjutant General of the British forces in South Africa until 1811. In his time there he earned a reputation as a competent administrator during the confusion that followed the British capture of the colony from the Dutch. When he replaced Lieutenant-Colonel Davey in April 1816, there was some hope that he would justify his reputation by restoring order and organisation to the government of the colony.

By the time Sorell was in charge in Van Diemen's Land, bushranging had almost become an open revolt and the convicts were practically out of control. In just over a year Sorell had organised the destruction of major bushranging groups and their supporters, leaving him free to carry out the reforms he had in mind.

He developed a system of control over the convicts through regular musters, the strict issue of passes and a series of registers. He built convict barracks in Hobart in 1822 and assigned prisoners to employers of good standing only. He also reserved tickets-of-leave to convicts with a history of good behaviour. In addition, Sorell established the brutal penal settlement of Sarah Island in the remote Macquarie Harbour.

A valuable administrator, after the unsuitable 'mates' who had filled the position before, Sorell's skills helped the future Tasmania become a profitable community with an exporting product base.

His private life gave his enemies ammunition against him, but even they objected when he was dismissed. Sorell died in London in 1848 — the Year of Revolutions.

The judge

Sir Redmond Barry was called to the Irish Bar in 1838. One of his closest friends in Dublin was Isaac Butt, founder of the Irish Home Rule movement. Barry was recognised as a kindly, social man but the Irish Bar was overstocked and he left for Australia in 1839. By no means a killjoy, Barry spent part of his passage confined to his cabin by the captain because he didn't keep his affair with a married woman passenger enough of a secret. He was admitted to the Sydney Bar in October of that year before moving on to Melbourne where he spent the rest of his life.

When Barry arrived in Melbourne he worked in the inferior (lower level) courts. On the first day of the first sittings of the Supreme Court of Melbourne — 12 April 1841 — Barry was admitted to practice and in 1851, when Victoria was firmly established as a separate colony, Barry was appointed its first Solicitor-General. He would go on to become Senior Puisne Judge of the Supreme Court of Victoria until his death.

Barry was a competent and conservative judge. He participated in debates about the general administration of the law in Victoria, the quality of the Supreme Court library, and the design of the new court buildings in William Street. In criminal cases he had a reputation for harshness, yet he supported the Discharged Prisoners' Aid Society and believed in the importance of rehabilitation. He saw Victoria as a frontier area where the law was not yet respected.

Remembered mainly for his judgements on Henry Garrett, the Eureka rebels, the convicts accused of the murder of John Price, and Ned Kelly, his work as an unofficial lawyer for Aborigines and his general interest in such matters as Aboriginal welfare are generally put aside. A public benefactor and supporter of the arts and the law, Barry died in November 1880, twelve days after the execution of Ned Kelly.

CONCLUSION

Over the 80 years of transportation, 162,000 convicts were set down on the Australian continent. The majority lived through their time and moved on to build new lives, but for some bolting was the only way.

Why did bolting come to an end? Who knows, maybe it didn't. Perhaps the results were less dramatic and nobody cared very much. Perhaps anyone who bolted in later years had a more sophisticated environment to disappear into. Perhaps the advent of communications and transport changes, and the development of more sophisticated policing methods, led to its demise. Or maybe it was just another of those passing fancies that fit their own times and none other.

Whichever way you look at it, the convict-bushrangers made life difficult for a society trying to create itself. But for the poorer free settlers, who felt the assumed superiority of other groups made life hard in a strange new world, the defiance shown by the bushrangers turned them into heroes.

Life was tough in the convict world, but so was the life they left behind. Discipline was based on the rules of the army and navy, but they were not always obeyed by those in authority. Governor Lachlan Macquarie ordered that no more than 50 lashes be the regular punishment — and that must have been obeyed at some time because a few sources refer to bolters who gave themselves up as being willing to 'take the 50' rather than

magistrates: persons authorised to try and sentence those accused without a jury

martinet: a stern and compulsive disciplinarian

New South Wales: originally all of settled Australia, but now a state

overseer: supervisor of convicts — often an ex-convict

pardons: a person granted an absolute pardon was free to leave the colony if he wished; a conditional pardon meant technical freedom but the person could not leave the colony until the term of the original sentence was completed

penal settlement: a community established specifically as a place of punishment

pickpocket: a sneak thief who 'dips' into pockets and bags for wallets, purses and money

plaited shirt: a shirt with a pleated front

posse: a group of people temporarily holding legal authority

powder: gunpowder

reprieved: have one's punishment cancelled or reduced

road gang: convicts chained together while working

scourger: a flogger, often very experienced

settlers: people who came to Australia for a new life, who usually settled on farms

sly grog: illegally produced and sold alcoholic drink

snuff-coloured: a dark yellow-brown colour, like powdered tobacco or snuff, that was usually inhaled

specials: men appointed as constables for a short time or emergency

***terra nullius*:** a Latin term meaning 'empty land'. It refers to a 17th century doctrine that described land unclaimed by a state or land that was not owned at all

'the 50': the 50 lashes declared to be sufficient punishment by Governor Lachlan Macquarie

ticket-of-leave: a convict permitted to live and work independently for himself until the end of his original sentence or until a pardon was granted; a ticket-of-leave could be revoked

transportation: banishment from one's current home to a foreign penal settlement

trooper: a soldier or police officer on horseback

Van Diemen's Land: the original name for Tasmania until 1856

whaleboat: a strong rowboat useful for quick control in rough seas

BIBLIOGRAPHY

Official documents

'A despatch from C J La Trobe Esq. to Earl Grey: the present state and prospects of the convicts in Van Diemen's Land (in Brand, Convict Probation System qv)'.

'Letters from Victorian Premiers', ed T F Bride. (Letter of T Chirnside, 1839).

'The Bigge Reports Facsimile edition', Libraries Board of South Australia, Adelaide, 1966.

Books

Primary sources

'A bloodthirsty banditti of wretches: informations on oath relating to Michael Howe and others between 1814 and 1818', *Historical Records of Australia*, (3rd series, vol 2) etc, Sullivan's Cove, Adelaide, 1985.

Cash, Martin, *Adventures of Martin Cash: comprising a faithful account of his exploits, while a bushranger under arms in Tasmania, in company with Kavanagh and Jones in the year 1843*, ed James Lester Burke, Hobart Town, 'Mercury' Steam Press Office, 1870.

Clark, C M H (ed), *Selected Documents in Australian History 1788–1850*, Angus & Robertson, Sydney, 1950.

Nicholls, Mary (ed), *Traveller Under Concern: the Quaker journals of Frederick Mackie on his tour of the Australasian Colonies 1852–1855*, University of Tasmania, Hobart, 1973.

Secondary sources

Acts of Bushranging, Apprehensions of Offenders 1862–1865, (series: Popinjay Publications' documents and facsimiles), Popinjay Publications, Canberra, 1988.

Ames, Delano (trans), *Larousse Encyclopedia of Modern History: from 1500 to the present day*, Hamlyn, London, 1974.

Barker, Anthony, *What Happened When: a chronology of Australia from 1788*, rev ed 2000, Allen and Unwin, Sydney, 2000.

Birch, Alan and Macmillan, David S, *The Sydney Scene 1788–1960*, Melbourne University Press, Melbourne, 1962.

Boldrewood, Rolf, *Robbery Under Arms*, Macmillan, Sydney, 1961 [1882].

Boxall, George, *An Illustrated History of Australian Bushrangers*, Viking (Penguin Books), Melbourne, 1988.

Brand, Ian (ed. M Sprod) *The Convict Probation System, Van Diemen's Land 1839–1854: a study of the probation system of convict discipline, together with C J La Trobe's 1847 report on its operation and the 1845 report of James Boyd on the probation station at Darlington, Maria Island,* Blubber Head Press, Hobart, 1990.

— *Port Arthur 1830–1877*, Jason Publications, West Moonah, 1975.

— *Penal Peninsula: Port Arthur and its outstations, 1827–1898*, Jason Publications, West Moonah, 1978.

— *Macquarie Harbour Penal Settlements 1822–1833 and 1846–1847*, Jason Publications, West Moonah, 1984.

Brissenden, Alan, *Rolf Boldrewood* (series: *Australian writers and their work*), Oxford University Press, Melbourne, 1972.

Bruce, Jill B, *Bushrangers: heroes, victims or villains?*, Kangaroo Press, Sydney, 2003.

Butler, Richard, *And Wretches Hang: the true and authentic story of the rise and fall of Matt Brady, bushranger*, Hyland House, Melbourne, 1977.

Clune, Frank, *The Norfolk Island Story*, Angus and Robertson, 1967.

Davey, G B and Seal, G (eds), *The Oxford Companion to Australian Folklore*, Oxford University Press, Melbourne, 1993.

Deane, Phyllis M, *The First Industrial Revolution*, Cambridge University Press, Cambridge, 1965.

Dick, George, *Bushranger of Bungendore*, Bungendore Historical Society, Bungendore, 1979.

Disher, Gary, *Wretches and Rebels: the Australian bushrangers* (series

Inquiring into Australian history), Oxford University Press, Melbourne, 1981.

Dugan, Michael, *Bushrangers* (series *Australian fact finders*), Macmillan, Melbourne, 1978.

Foster, Elizabeth, *Australia's First Settlement*, Oxford University Press, Melbourne, 1987.

Gard, Stephen, *Bushrangers*, Reed Education (Heinemann), Melbourne, 1997.

Graham, Pamela, *End of an Era*, (series: *Australia's bushrangers*), Macmillan Education Australia, Melbourne, 1999.

— *Bail Up!* (series: *Australia's bushrangers*), Macmillan Education Australia, Melbourne, 1999.

— *The Bolters* (series: *Australia's bushrangers*), Macmillan Education Australia, Melbourne, 1999.

— *Hanged, Shot or Exiled* (series: *Australia's bushrangers*), Macmillan Education Australia, Melbourne, 1999.

— *Felons on the Run* (series: *Australia's bushrangers*), Macmillan Education Australia, Melbourne, 1999.

Jones, Graham, *Bushrangers of the North East*, Charquin Hill Publishing, Wangaratta, 1991.

Joy, William and Prior, Tom, *Bushrangers*, Rigby, Sydney, 1971.

Julien, Robert, *Bail up the Phoenix*, Jacobyte Books, Mitcham, 2002.

Laidlaw, Ronald, *Australian History*, Macmillan Education Australia, Melbourne, 1991.

MacFie, Peter H, 'Point Puer boy' establishment, Van Diemen's Land (Tas): the first 68 boys', *Tasmania History Studies*, vol 6, no 2, 1999.

McLachlan, Iaen, *Place of Banishment: Port Macquarie 1818–1832*, Hale & Iremonger, Sydney, 1988.

McLachlan, R, *Handbook for the Point Puer database 'the Point Puer lads'*, Mitchell College of Advanced Education, Bathurst, 1985.

Molitorisz, Sacha, *Australian Bushrangers: the romance of robbery*, Harcourt Education, Sydney, 2003.

Nixon, Allan M, *100 Australian Bushrangers 1789–1901*, Rigby, Adelaide, 1982.

Norman, L, *Sea Wolves and Bandits: sealing, whaling, smuggling and piracy, wild men of Van Diemen's Land, bushrangers and bandits, wrecks and wreckers: with a chronology of curious and interesting facts relating to old Van Diemen's Land and (from 1856) to Tasmania*, Walch, Hobart, 1946.

Perry, T M, *Australia's First Frontier: the spread of settlement in New South Wales 1788–1829*, Melbourne University Press in association with the Australian National University, Melbourne, 1963.

Pow, Graham, *Barefoot Bandit: the story of Tom Hughes, West Australian bushranger*, G Pow, Maylands, 2003.

Rienits, Rex and Thea, *A Pictorial History of Australia*, Hamlyn London, 1969.

Robinson, Portia, *The Women of Botany Bay: a reinterpretation of the role of women in the origins of Australian society*, The Macquarie Library, Sydney, 1988.

Scott, Bill, *Australian Bushrangers*, Child & Henry Publishing, Sydney, 1987.

Tate, J E, *Convicts* (series: *Discovering Australian history*), Jacaranda Press, Brisbane, 1970.

Taylor, Peter, *The Bushrangers*, Shakespeare Head Press, Oxford, 1983.

van Asten, David, *Bushrangers*, Lamont Books, Melbourne, 1986.

van Oudtshoorn, Nic (series ed), *Australian History School Projects: The first fleet and convicts*, Maximedia, Jamberoo, 2002.

Waddell, Helen, *ABC of Australian Bushrangers and Criminals: an index to the story of the Australian bushranger by George E Boxall*, [ca 1907].

Williams, Stephan, *Book of a Thousand Bushrangers*, Popinjay Publications, Canberra, 1993.

— *The Annals of Bushranging in the Colony of NSW*, Popinjay Publications, Canberra, 1994.

Wright, Reg, *The Forgotten Generation of Norfolk Island and Van Diemen's Land*, Library of Australian History, Sydney, 1986.

Websites

(Accessed between 29 May and 10 July 2006)

www.abc.net.au/rn/talks/8.30/lawrpt/lstories/lr160103.htm

http://adb.anu.edu.au/

http://www.australiahistory.com.au/

http://australiaonthemap.org.au

http://www.blaxland.com/ozships/http://cedir.uow.edu.au/programs/
FirstFleet/

http://www.convictcreations.com/history/crimes.htm

http://www.discovertasmania.com.au/

http://www.dnzb.govt.nz/dnzb/default.asp?Find_Quick.asp?Person
Essay=1C9

http://gutenberg.net.au/search.html

http://www.hotkey.net.au/~jwilliams4/cons.htm

http://www.nla.gov.au/ferg/

http://www.nla.gov.au/ozlife

http://members.iinet.net.au/~perthdps/convicts/res-12.html

http://www.whiskershill.dynamite.com.au/b.htm

http://www.portarthur.org.au/

www.records.nsw.gov.au/indexes/colsec/default.htm

http://scs.une.edu.au/Bushrangers/biog.htm

http://www.trinity.wa.edu.au/plduffyrc/subjects/sose/austhist/bush/
default.htm

INDEX